KU-607-354

CONTENTS

ACKNOWLEDGEMENTS

Even before the process of writing this book began, there were people who showed belief and encouragement, in me and my tale.

At the beginning I didn't see it. From my point of view I had just mucked up, should serve my time and be quiet, but from their point of view I had a story to tell that could be useful to others.

Jason Radcliffe was the first of them, he has been nothing short of inspirational: always seeing the positive in every situation. Quite simply this book would not have existed without him. Thank you Jason for your friendship and support.

Guy Woodward; there is no one who has championed the Chris Lewis cause more than Guy, his desire to help a friend who had fallen has been an example in caring. Thanks to you and your beautiful wife Jean, you are both wonderful people.

Also thanks to Judith Lewis, Ashley Brown, Gordon Chetwood and Tim Clamp, for proofreading and all of the meetings. Your help is very much appreciated.

Special thanks to Patricia Fearon, Mark Lewis and Bashir; your contribution cannot be put into words, except one – love.

Finally, thanks goes out to the publishers of this book, The History Press. Mark Beynon was sure that he wanted to publish this story and with the help of Lauren Newby we got there in the end. Thank you for your patience.

CRAZY
MY ROAD TO REDEMPTION

CHRIS LEWIS

with Jed Pitman

The
History
Press

First published 2017, this edition published 2018

The History Press
The Mill, Brimscombe Port
Stroud, Gloucestershire, GL5 2QG
www.thehistorypress.co.uk

British Library Cataloguing in Publication Data.
A catalogue record for this book is available from the British Library.

ISBN 978 0 7509 8695 3
Typesetting and origination by The History Press
Printed and bound by CPI Group (UK) Ltd

1

THE ARREST

I've never been so apprehensive in my life. It's Monday 8 December 2008. My Virgin Airways plane lands from St Lucia into the South Terminal of Gatwick Airport. It's just after eight o'clock in the morning.

I've arrived and I'm scared. While my fellow travellers nervously grip their partners' hands in anticipation of the first violent contact with the tarmac, all I can think of are the cans of fruit juice in my luggage that contain cocaine. Paranoia seeps from the air vents and heightens all my emotions. I'm unsure of what's real or what's not. Everyone appears to be looking at me with accusing eyes.

There's a family occupying a row further along the fuselage, and when the father looking around the cabin turns in my direction, I'm sure that this brief eye contact is a tacit accusation. He seems to look at me with an accusing eye, but how can he know? Maybe he's a police officer and is keeping an eye on me, because they already know. Paranoia is going to be the theme of the whole morning.

The airport at this time of day is quiet. I walk to passport control and there are two men standing behind the counter. I assume they're checking all the travellers, but they seem to be looking directly at me and no one else. I walk through passport control to the baggage reclaim area, where bags are slowly beginning to emerge from the carousel flaps. Many cases travel the full circle a number of times, while others are claimed immediately by their owners, who then head to customs. For a while, there's no sign of my bag. It seems like an eternity, but then my luggage emerges from behind the plastic strips. I look at my bag nervously. It's slightly ajar, the zipper half open. I hadn't put any padlocks on them. But then again, I'm very tired and realise that in my many years of travelling I've often failed to close my bag properly. 'Come on, Chris, pull yourself together. You're just overthinking everything,' I tell myself. I look around and pick up my bag, taking a deep breath. I follow a group of fellow passengers towards the 'nothing to declare' exit. They walk through but before I can reach the exit one of the officers I thought had been looking at me earlier is now standing there. His voice is calm and level as he says, 'Excuse me, sir, may I check your luggage?' My bag is taken to one side and the officer looks through it. He reaches for the three cans of fruit juice and removes them. Inside, I'm shaking, trembling. I can hardly stand.

The officer takes the cans to be X-rayed. His body language betrays nothing as he lifts the cans and places them on the X-ray machine. In an instant, I have a thousand thoughts that trigger the infinite consequences of my actions. I try to breathe more slowly. The officer returns and tells me that the X-rays have revealed nothing. A sense of relief washes over me, but it's only momentary as he explains that he is going to have to open the cans. Around me normal life carries on as people chat on their way back from various destinations, but I feel disconnected from it, as if in a bubble of my own anxiety. The first sobering thoughts I've had in months become so obvious and apparent, and when the officer returns, having discovered the cocaine, I know that everything is going to change. In an instant, the future looks very different to the one I had imagined. The officer takes the cans away and for a brief time I am alone. For a second or two, I almost convince myself that everything is going to be okay, but it passes before I can blink, as reality floods in and drowns out any sense of hope. 'What's my mum going to say?' 'What are my brothers going to think?' 'What about the press and everyone else?' No part of this is going to be good. The customs officer returns after what could have been minutes or seconds – I don't know. He tells me the cans have tested positive for cocaine. Doom and gloom descends. He asks me to follow him. I am taken upstairs and to the left, into what looks like a normal waiting room. At this time, I can't say I'm even thinking anymore. I can feel the panic running through my body. Externally, I try to remain calm, but inside I'm racing. I'm like the duck that seems at ease on the water while underneath its legs are going crazy. I'm waiting for the police to arrive, and when they do, I am arrested. So begins a long journey, one that would take six-and-a-half years of my life.

I arrive at Brighton police station. I don't remember much of the journey. At the station, I'm processed and put into a cell. My mind continues to race. In the cell, I'm alone for the first time. My head is spinning, I could scream with disbelief about where I am. A while later, I'm told that I can make my phone call. There is no doubt who I am going to call – my younger brother, Mark, but then I remember he'll be at work and unable to take the call, so I choose a close friend instead. I ask them to tell my brother where I am and what has happened – that I've been arrested.

My night in Brighton police station is just surreal. It's hard to comprehend quite how I've moved from one state of being to another so rapidly. A few hours before, I had been a free man returning home. Now, I'm a criminal facing a long sentence in jail and have to tell my loved ones not just where I am, but what I have done. I spend one night in Brighton before I'm taken to a prison in Surrey. Driving into the prison, I recall all the prison movies I had seen as a younger man. We all have a vision of what prison must be like, and I'm about to experience mine first hand. This is so far out of my comfort zone, I can't believe it.

I doubt whether I can survive even a couple of days in here. I don't think so. With the cell door locked behind me, it's the first time in a long while that things are quiet. I think about my family, but it only makes my head spin and I want to scream.

When I decided to import drugs I never gave my family a thought. I didn't think about the negative aspects of what I was about to do. I was never going to be caught, so I never had to think about the consequences for my family. Now in this cell they come to mind. What have I done? I sit and think about the countless others who are going to be affected by the fallout from this. My family and friends are going to be affected and that's hard to cope with because, although I will have to live with my mistakes, they will inadvertently have to share some of this with me as well.

The moment I start to think about those close to me, what I have done really begins to hit home. Nobody can knock on my door now, but others will be doing that to the people I care about. I have just added to their burden. As the elder son and brother, it was always my job to protect my family and I have just failed spectacularly.

2

REMAND

I emerge bleary-eyed into my first morning of incarceration at HMP High Down in Surrey. As I sit in my cell, all my thoughts are negative and I seriously doubt whether I can cope with this new reality. Simple things that I normally take for granted, like the liberty of walking down the street, are at the forefront of my mind. I yearn for the simple things, not thought about in decades. The truth is that I already know it will be some time before I experience normality again. The best-case scenario is that I'll get bail while the prosecution prepares its case.

My solicitor arrives and tells me that the application for bail will take a couple of weeks. Even a fortnight now seems like a lifetime. I guess I'll just have to cope as best I can. Two weeks – surely I have the mental strength to get through that short period. Over those couple of weeks I must have cut a sorry figure. That's the emotional stress. I'm in new territory and I have no skill set to deal with this. I say very little, there is nothing to say, but I'm trying hard to remain positive.

Within days I get a job serving food to other inmates, which gives me something to do three times a day. This job allows me to get out of my cell, which is important, as without the work I could be locked up for twenty-three hours a day. The activity helps the day pass more quickly and has the added benefit of me getting more food, so I don't feel as hungry. I've never been the fattest of people, and keeping my weight up has often been something I've had to watch. In here, within a couple of days, the weight just falls off.

As well as my work in the kitchen I try to occupy myself further by wearing a second hat. I become a 'foreign rep', which basically means I go to see new foreign nationals coming into the jail. I ask them about their needs and help them to navigate their way through the criminal system, which I too am learning. Even in the state my mind is in, it's quite easy to see and appreciate that there are people here who are in a worse predicament than myself – people who don't speak English and therefore find it hard to understand how the system works. I try to make it easier for them. I also spend some of my time as an anti-bullying rep, anything to keep the grey matter working. Bullying within the prison service is a big no-no. I'm paid £1 per day for the servery work; the other tasks are unpaid but they keep me busy.

Although I'm on remand, having only just been arrested, I'm treated like all the other prisoners. The days pass in a routine way, as you would expect in such an institution. My cell is unlocked early and I begin serving at 8 a.m. for about forty minutes, after which time I tidy, wash up and generally help out. Afterwards I have my own breakfast, which is usually cereal or toast, except at weekends when we might have a cooked breakfast. Most days serving breakfast is over by 10 a.m. unless there's a deep clean of the kitchen, which gives me a short time to fill before the lunch serving. I'm then back in my cell until the evening meal at 6 p.m. I spend that time reading and trying not to think, as any activity is better than dwelling on my predicament.

When I can, I walk around the wing or go to the gym. It's a blessing that my serving job provides me with something on which to focus and the opportunity to be out of my cell for longer periods.

At night, there is no hiding in routine and activity, and so the nightmares come. It is quite simple: I am afraid. Fear is a part of life, but this is just too big a fear to deal with. In fact, it's more than one fear, it's a host of them. One nightmare involves me trying to get away, but from what I can never tell. I'm trying to get my groove on and run very fast, but instead I'm running in slow motion like Steve Austin in *The Six Million Dollar Man*. In another I am up high in a precarious position, like on the edge of a crane, with the wind howling around me. I never fall but I'm always scared that I will. As the time passes, I learn that I'm never going to fall, but this does not remove the fear; all I can see stretching into the distance is day after day of the same nightmares. Yet, through all of this, on the exterior I still try to remain as calm and polite as possible, even though my nightmares tell me that I am absolutely bricking it. There is a moment just before I open my eyes when I can allow myself to believe that I'm in my own bed, in my own house, and that prison was all some terrible dream. But then I open my eyes and the cell is still there. I realise with dread that this nightmare is real.

I may be occupied doing something with my mind, but there is still a horrible feeling of unease that is always there, right by my side. I can't get shot of it, whatever I try. I am not always consciously thinking about what the unease is, but it's always there. In a matter of days, I'm already noticing that I've become a lot greyer. I had one or two grey hairs before, but now they're increasing rapidly.

This all goes on for the two weeks while I wait for news of my immediate future. Finally, I receive the date of my bail hearing. When it comes, I must face the immediate disappointment that I'm not going to leave prison for my day in court, as the hearing will be via videophone.

I am taken to a room where my future will be decided. Many others have been in this room today, some were successful and some not. But I'm hopeful I'll get bail, and with it a little space in my head, temporarily at least. I watch for half an hour while the two sides of the argument are given. The State is arguing that I'm a flight risk, but I suppose that depends on how you would describe a flight risk, as I reckon I could only make it outside this room before someone recognises me at this moment. But I'm not the master of things to come, I gave that up when I broke the law. The nameless faces of the jury retire to decide my fate. While I wait, I stare at the empty chairs. I am devastated – they say I'm a flight risk. The hope that had sustained me through the first two weeks evaporates in an instant and I want to scream, but I have to bottle it up, as it won't help. I must try to focus and get my head around this.

Expressing my disappointment would serve no purpose. There are plenty of people in this prison who have been sentenced and are facing many years — even life — yet they find a way to cope. I have never considered myself weak so there must be a way for me to cope. These inmates are an example but not an inspiration; my aim is to reapply for bail in a month and to get it right next time. So, it's back to setting that goal and working towards it — just another month.

Time passes relatively quickly. It is something of a contradiction: the days seem to pass so slowly, but the months flash by. I decide that this is because jail is full of routine and drudgery so that, looking back, it is very hard to separate one day from another, as each day is filled with uneventful regularity. For forty years, whatever problems I had, I could at least walk out the door and go where I wished, but that privilege is no longer mine. It's a strange feeling, knowing that I can no longer make those choices. All this puts the previous problems in my life in perspective and I realise that what I thought were major issues were actually insignificant ones.

I know I must find a way to cope in prison and believe that things will get better. All the choices were mine and only I am responsible for my incarceration. I could be in prison for fifteen years — it almost takes my breath away thinking about that — so the sooner I get used to that, the better. I'm not dwelling on how I got here and why I made the choices that led to my arrest. You may ask, 'Why not?' Well, if you fall into a river and get swept along by the current, you don't think, 'I wonder what caused me to slip?' You think, 'How the fuck am I going to get out of here?' Once the immediate fear has gone, then you might go back to find out why and how you fell in, but not right now. That said, these questions would start to form later. Right here and now, I have more pressing things in my head – mainly my current predicament. I need to deal with that before I'm even capable of thinking about how I fell off the bridge into the river.

My fear has created a view of my experience that is at odds with reality. We tend to get our view of prison from TV and movies and there are things that go on in jail that are mirrored in fiction.

However, it's not as bad as the movies would have you believe. Prison is not supposed to be a pleasant experience, it is a punishment after all, and it's definitely not like Butlin's, as some would have you believe. Okay, I have a TV in my room, but that doesn't compensate for not having your freedom or being able to spend time with your loved ones. I understand that I made the choices that put me in here, but that doesn't make my situation any more comfortable or pleasant.

I receive my first visit. It's my brother, Mark, and I have no idea what I can say to him. Saying 'I'm sorry' at this point seems weak and pointless. I guess it's one of those situations where I'll have to sit here and accept whatever comes. It's a very difficult visit. Sitting in front of Mark, my fear doesn't seem to be as important and, for a moment, it's gone.

As a young boy, my desire to set a good example for Mark has helped me greatly in my career – the fact that he was present and watching what I did drove me to work harder. That makes me feel even worse now. I cringe when I think of the size of my failure. Mark reports back to my mum that I'm okay, but that I was constantly rubbing my head, and they all know that's what I do when I am stressed. It occurs to me that all visits could be as emotionally charged as this one, and a visit from my mum even more so. Thinking of her is very difficult and I know that I don't have the words to explain how I feel, or to begin to explain why I made the choices I did.

When I see my family, I'm filled with an overwhelming feeling of disappointment in myself for what I've done to them. But still, they come, and I am so pleased to see them. Despite my guilt, nobody points an accusatory finger and no one asks why. They just seem to instinctively know how I am feeling and support me.

My friends also begin to visit and, finally, after weeks of incarceration, I laugh. Because they are mates they ask me things that a family member doesn't and it's something of a relief to be able to do that. I can tell them how it is in here and that, in spite of everything, I'm okay.

My mates and I have been through a lot – grown up together, got in trouble together – and so to them this is just another scrape, albeit a more serious one. But we can talk. They ask if I did it, and there's no judgement – that's a comfort. We talk about how we dealt with situations we had been in in the past, trying to find some positivity from difficulties we overcame, and we remind ourselves that we have coped with things before. We all understand that this is much bigger, but the principle is the same. So, focus remains my mantra: find any peace or positivity and focus on that.

Back in my new world, my final application for bail is denied. I didn't prepare myself for this but I seem to be coping better. I'm not as devastated. I simply set my internal clock for the next four months ahead to my trial. I find out my case is going to be heard on Monday 17 May.

I go from being 'the accused' to being a convicted criminal. The judge sentences me to thirteen years in prison. Thirteen years! I look over at my brother Liam, tears in his eyes. He comes close to the cage and I tell him to take care of our mother. I'm now worried about what I may have done to her health.

Very quickly I'm back downstairs in the cells. It's been hard trying to describe the emotions of being sentenced to thirteen years in jail – the fear of what's to come, the disappointment in myself, the pain I've caused my loved ones, and not having the opportunity to make things better for many years. These thoughts seem to come all at once. Shit, it's all too much. It's like, it's happening, but it can't be happening. Such a weird state, disbelief I guess.

3

THE YOUNG AND INNOCENT CHRIS LEWIS

It was Friday 10 March 1978, just after 10 a.m., and I had just landed in London from Guyana. It was my first time on a plane; so I'd stayed in my seat the entire flight. I didn't understand how anything around me worked. I was venturing into a new world, one that would change my life forever. I was neither perturbed nor frightened: this was an adventure for the 10-year-old Chris. I had left my home in Guyana to come and live with my mother and father in England, the start of a new life away from my friends. It was the kind of journey travelled by many black people at that time.

My mum and my Aunt Hazel came to collect me. My feet were hurting and my very smart suit was a little tight, since it had been made for me a few months earlier and I had grown. My aunt picked me up and carried me through the airport, beyond the thousands of people that were arriving and leaving. I had never seen anything like it. Everything was so big and so different. When I had imagined the streets of London, they were all paved with gold, and everything else in a similar hue. Yet I was greeted with this blanket grey that seemed to head from the ground to the sky, with nothing else in between.

The following day, I woke at my aunt's house in Harlesden, where my mum had been living. There was a chill in the air that I had never experienced before, but at least there was one thing I could do that would bring me back to normality – I could find a radio and listen to some cricket. Once I had tracked down a radio, I started trying to tune into the station I had listened to back in Guyana. I spent hours trying to fine-tune the radio to find the cricket. At first, I just couldn't understand why it wasn't there.

I did this for the first week I spent in England. No cricket – this was going to be hard. I realised that I wasn't enjoying my new home. I spent a lot of time missing Guyana and my gran, desperate for some familiarity.

Ah, my gran. Back in Guyana, everyone was brought up with traditional British values, with discipline at the forefront; after all, the country had been a British colony for 150 years until 1966. My job as a small boy was simple: I had to go to school, behave myself and be well mannered – be seen and not heard. I certainly never answered back to my elders, not that I was always the best behaved. As a young boy, I spent a lot of time outdoors with my friends, playing cricket, climbing trees and teasing the local dogs so that they would chase us. Some of this behaviour got us into trouble. We were pretty fearless at that stage, only the fearing the anger of our mums. One of the things my mother taught me was not to follow others; but, like all kids, I would do just that. My mum quickly put a stop to it and she wouldn't accept any excuses. She would ask me, 'If your friends jumped off a bridge, would you?' The answer would, of course, be no and that would be that.

Our home was filled with music and my first ever memory is of my mum dancing. I wanted her to pick me up but she was enjoying herself, so I began to cry – crying seemed to be a response to just about everything when I was 2 years old – but moments later my Aunt Hazel had lifted me up and I was flying through the air and all was good in my world once again.

Our family was an extended one, the head of which was my grandmother, Eunice. We grew up in Agricola on the outskirts of Georgetown, Guyana, in South America. I was born there on 14 February 1968. Our community was a mixed community, one made up predominantly of West Indians and East Indians, along with a sprinkling of Chinese and Portuguese people.

My father, Philip, had left to join his mother in England soon after I was born. Back then people saved up to emigrate to America, Canada or Britain, usually one member of the family at a time, looking for a better life. In the Caribbean in those days, the whole idea of England and Englishness was idolised; it was the pinnacle of everything. England was seen as a land of opportunity and I knew from an early age that I would be going there.

My gran had ten children: four boys (my uncles James, Wilfred, Colin and Michael) and six girls (my mum, Patricia, and my aunts Princess, Hazel, Marine, Juliette and Cleopatra). Princess died before I was born, so I grew up with nine of my gran's offspring all in the same house, along with my grandma, her partner, my sister Vanessa, and my cousins Susan and Felix. Large, extended families were pretty much the norm for our community.

Uncle James was a carpenter. He did carpentry around the house and made figures and decorative maps out of wood to literally carve out a living. Then there was my Uncle Wilfred. He had been in the army before becoming a tailor. A good-looking man with a big Afro, he wore high heels and an open shirt showing off a medallion. He was so cool, the coolest guy around at the time, and I wanted to be just like him.

Much of Guyana is below sea level and Gran's wooden house, like most houses here, was built on stilts. At the front there were stairs that took you up to a veranda where you could sit outside. There were four bedrooms: at night there would be three or four in the bed and some on the floor, but this was normal. If you had a large family, whether your house had two bedrooms or just the one, that was how people lived. This might remind some people of the conditions of the Bucket family in Roald Dahl's *Charlie and the Chocolate Factory*.

At the back was the kitchen. There was electricity, but we cooked on gas from cylinders. In Guyana, you had to know how to do things. We kept chickens, and from time to time my gran would ask my uncle to catch a chicken and do the necessary – chop its head off and pluck the feathers. When they were feeling particularly mischievous, they would break a chicken's neck and watch it run around for a while. Then we would build a fire and cook the bird outside.

As a young boy, I would watch what they were doing; by the time I was 5, I could build my own fire and cook outdoors. I used two concrete bricks, one at each end, to support a metal sheet that I would cook on. Then I would put the wood underneath, light the fire and put the pot on top. These were the things I had to learn when I was a young boy growing up. All of us had to be, to some extent, self-sufficient. That was the way of the world for us.

There was no running water indoors, so in the morning we had to go and fetch our own water from a pump at the end of the road to have a shower. From the time I could stand, I went and got my own water. This was very normal for our community; we were all being prepared for later life. In this environment, there was no social security or handouts. If you couldn't do it yourself, it wouldn't get done. If everyone was proactive and you weren't, you stood out like a sore thumb.

So, as a young boy, I learned to cook, clean and sew, and I was even handy with a cutlass, which we used to cut the grass in the back garden. Having said that, one day, while I was being a bit carefree with the cutlass, I nearly chopped off one of my toes. It was hanging on by the skin but somehow it managed to reattach itself, as if by magic. Losing a toe would have had a disastrous effect on my future career as a fast bowler. Another time I jumped out of a tree without noticing a stake sticking up out of the ground and it went right through my foot.

While I don't remember being ill, my childhood contained plenty of other mishaps – or, as I would call them, learning experiences. I was once run over on the road outside my house, but I don't recall a thing. I was 5 or 6 years old at the time and I do remember waking up in hospital and looking around and thinking, 'What's going on?' I was just about to panic when I looked out of the window and saw my gran coming into the hospital. My last recollection had been of playing happily the day before. A day and a half was completely lost and I have never been able to recall the accident. Apparently, I was standing on the wooden bridge over the little river that led to our garden when a car reversed and hit me.

I must admit that I do find that very strange. When we were kids, we were running around outside all the time. We weren't slow, and I would have thought it unlikely that a reversing car could have caught me unawares. We were constantly aware of traffic, as we were already playing cricket a lot in the road and had to move our stuff out of the way to let the cars go by, although, there were few cars in our road. I thought to myself, 'Were you sleeping? How did you not see or hear a car coming onto the bridge?' But that's the story. To this day, the after-effects of the accident bring on occasional headaches and eye aches.

I was 7 or 8 when I first went to visit one of my aunts, who had moved into a relatively new complex. She had the first flushing toilet I had ever seen. We had an old outhouse and if you looked down you would see a year's worth of shit.

The houses in the area were pretty well spread out. There was no real plan. When someone had a piece of land, they built on it and every house looked different. Some people could only afford a certain amount of building material, so if they didn't have enough money they would have to wait until the next time they got paid, then they would buy more materials to finish off the house. Some houses took many years to complete.

There were two mango trees in our front garden and other fruit trees around the side and back. These gave us star apples (a sweet, black fruit), gooseberries, carambola (also known as 'five finger fruits' in Guyana), awara, sapodilla and breadfruit.

Looking back now, people had a hard life in Guyana in the 1960s and '70s, but we didn't perceive it as such. You couldn't get potatoes or some tinned goods due to a ban on certain imports. Forbes Burnham, the prime minister during that period, as a student in London, had known Kwame Nkrumah of Ghana, Michael Manley of Jamaica and other political figures who went on to become leaders of newly independent countries of Africa and the Caribbean.

I remember the first time I saw an apple. My uncle brought one home; I don't know where he got it. He cut it up and shared it so that everyone could have a little taste. While I never went hungry, there were basic foodstuffs that you simply couldn't get.

My mum Patricia was young, fit and athletic, and, boy, could she run — bad news for me, as she could always catch me. Many times, I ran knowing that I was in trouble. I would get some way down the road before I felt her hands on my shoulders. Holding me with one hand, she would smack me with the other, while I did a little dance in a futile attempt to avoid the blows. I suppose it must have been comical to people watching, but if it was my turn today then it would be one of my friends tomorrow. This was fairly routine for young boys growing up in our community.

There was a massive oil refinery at the end of our street and sometimes we would find very large oil drums. Cut lengthways, we found that they floated quite well and could be used as a boat along the Demerara River; we did this with abandoned car tops as well. All the huge tankers used to come up the Demerara and we would paddle to the massive boats. This was probably not the best idea, particularly as none of us could swim – take on a little bit of water and it would have been all over.

Of course, with any prank like that, word got straight back to my mother. She would know what I had been up to before I got home and so there would inevitably be trouble. By the time I was only halfway home, I could hear my mum calling – oops, somebody had seen us! – and I could tell by the tone in her voice that she wasn't happy. I walked down Water Street contemplating my fate, knowing I had to go home. I went in and my mum came towards me and as usual I made a run for it. It wasn't long before she had caught up with me, but even I, at that young age, thought I was due for some punishment.

But by the time I was 8, I could run faster than my mum and she could no longer catch me. One day, I was making a run for it when I reached the point where she usually caught up with me, but this time she hadn't. I looked around and mum was standing in the middle of the road gasping, out of breath. It was the first time I had been able to get away.

I remember these moments with fondness and laughter. That young, feisty West Indian lady is, these days, wrapped around the fingers of each and every one of her grandchildren, nothing but gentleness left.

Discipline was firm in those days and, coupled with religious beliefs, this meant that as a child you were simply judged on how well you followed a grown-up's orders. My father was a preacher, so I had religion at home, but as he was often away my gran, a religious woman, picked up the reins. The Bible and its teachings were always close at hand.

School was intermittent, as I was taken out of school because I would soon be going to England. The entire education system was English. Everything you heard about England was great, so standards of discipline and good behaviour had to be high.

From an early age I was imbued with English values, and when I say English values, these were the perceived English values of the time. Although I feel very West Indian, many West Indians would think I was very English.

I remember my very first day at school where we all had to stand up and introduce ourselves to our classmates. I rose to my feet and announced that I was Clairmonte. The whole class laughed; 5-year-olds can be tough. By morning break, when questioned about my name again, it had miraculously changed to Chris, my middle name, which seemed more acceptable. From then on, I was always Chris.

Like most kids, I would sometimes try to bunk off school but my mum would have none of that and she would walk a few paces behind me to make sure I went. What I learned at school was not much different to my home life. At school the discipline was strict. If you turned up late you got a smack on the hand with a cane. This was supposed to encourage punctuality, which proved ironic considering how things turned out later in my life. If you misbehaved and it was serious enough, they wrote home to your mother. What you had done, essentially, was embarrass your mother in public, and she wasn't going to like that because it showed that she hadn't done her job properly. At the very least, she would give you a couple of slaps on the bottom with a slipper or a belt. You knew you would be disciplined and no one in the household would support you behaving badly at school.

Away from school, Mum would make the journey to Georgetown, 2 to 3 miles away, and occasionally I would go with her. Georgetown was a special place for me. There were so many people, different smells, lots of colours. It seemed much more alive and I loved the excitement of it. After mum had finished her shopping there would also be a treat, something I could not get in the village – fried chicken, fancy ice cream or even a new cricket ball. Some Fridays, my friends and I might even be able to go to the cinema. We would go to watch a kung fu movie and play-fight all the way home. But these were special occasions. The only thing that filled almost every waking moment, seven days a week, was cricket. My time out of class belonged to me. While the adults spent their time working or looking for work, we kids were told to go out and play. I would run around in my underwear, both in and out of the house, doing cartwheels, climbing trees and throwing stones at the birds perched on electrical lines. But I have simply loved cricket for as long as I can remember. From the moment I could stand, I played cricket. I played cricket before I went to school, during school and after school. In fact, going to school only interrupted me from playing cricket, as I would sit in class looking out of the window, daydreaming of playing cricket.

My life involved just two things: eating (when I was hungry, I climbed a fruit tree in our garden and ate) and playing cricket. The only thing cricket was dependent on was whether my friends and I could find a ball or make one using the tubes from bicycle tyres. To make the ball, we would get a seed of the awara plant, an edible fruit native to Guyana. The hard seed is about the size of a golf ball and we would wrap it in newspaper, keeping its round shape, before covering it with the cut rubber from the inner tube of a bicycle tyre to make a bouncy ball. Other times, we would just use a tin can, which would obviously become flat very quickly, especially as we always played on the streets and whacked the daylight out of it. Sometimes, one of my uncles would buy us a $5 rubber ball, but that would never last long either, as we would hit it into some bushes and lose the ball within five minutes. And you could hardly go back and ask for another $5.

The oil drums from the local refinery were used for many things. The lids of the drums, for example, became our wickets, propped up using a stick, and bats were made of slats from wooden fences. With a cutlass, we would cut it to size, then shape one end to make a handle. Later we learned to sand down the handle so we didn't get splinters, otherwise, you just got used to it. We had no gloves or pads so you had to watch the ball and make sure you didn't get hit, because if you did it wouldn't be pleasant. Remember, too, that we were playing in bare feet. So, cricket dominated my life from a very early age. The game was everywhere. None of the other kids were playing football or tennis, golf or rugby, it was just cricket. We would play it all the time and wherever we could.

I would avoid chores in order to play. One Saturday morning, I was playing cricket with my friends, having not helped with any of the household chores, when Uncle Wilfred saw what I was doing and said that he would be along in ten minutes to watch me play. He told me that if I didn't score at least twenty-five runs then there would be trouble. When he arrived I was batting, trying my hardest to make sure I scored the necessary runs, no playing across the line, no swiping. Wilfred joined in and batted at the other end but got out, leaving me on 8 not out. Because he left me stranded, he decided that my failure to achieve twenty-five was in part down to him. I was delighted. There were no harsh words for abandoning my chores and I could carry on playing. Cricket was already a big part in my life.

It was, of course, an ideal time to be in the Caribbean as a cricket lover, with the West Indies producing some amazingly talented players, the likes of whom we may never see again. As a community and a country, we all looked to the cricket team for inspiration and simply that feel-good factor. The great West Indian players of the time inspired a generation of kids who thought about nothing else – me amongst them.

We all listened to transistor radios at night when the West Indies were touring. I used to love hearing all about the opening batsmen, Roy Fredericks and Gordon Greenidge. It felt like every single ball they faced was hit for four, with Fredericks hooking everything that was bowled at him. It was so exciting listening to commentators Reds Perreira and Tony Cozier. They were so enthusiastic and brought everything to life; their commentary was like poetry. Before I came to England, my radio and I lived side-by-side when the cricket was on.

I used to honestly believe that the entire great West Indian team, which included Viv Richards, Alvin Kalicharran, Clive Lloyd, Larry Gomes, Michael Holding, Andy Roberts, Colin Croft, Bernard Julian and Joel Garner, were about 10ft tall. They must have been giants to be as good as they were.

I was a staunch West Indian supporter, but I learned about players from all over the world. The great names that stood out for me were Dennis Amiss, Geoff Boycott, Dennis Lillee, Jeff Thomson, the Chappell brothers, Zaheer Abbas, Sunil Gavaskar, Bishen Bedi – the list is endless. These were players I greatly admired; they did well against the West Indies and so were imprinted on my mind.

I knew all about these players and many more. I had listened time and time again to these guys scoring runs and taking wickets. In fact, such battles with these players were immortalised in song in Guyana. Here's a verse from one:

No bowler holds a terror for Vivian Richards
Not Thomson or Lillee, not Bedi or Chandrasekhar
Perfect coordination of body and mind, that brother is really dynamite
Pace or spin, he don't give a front what you are bowling him
Fast or slowly, you're going back to the boundary.

While I was desperate to follow in their footsteps, I never held a proper cricket bat or cricket ball until I came to England. Along with my friends, Lawrence and Shaun, we gave ourselves names when we were playing. Of course, everybody wanted to be Viv Richards, but an older boy called Sulka always got to be him, so I chose Greenidge instead. I spent a lot of my time as a child pretending to be Gordon Greenidge, although I had never seen him play.

Then, one day in early 1977 when I was 8 years old, I heard that Pakistan were touring the Caribbean and they were playing a three-day game against a Guyanese team. My gran paid for me to go up to Border to watch, but when I got to the cricket ground the game was sold out and I couldn't get in. I climbed one of the many trees that overlooked the ground and from there I watched part of the game. I was so excited, and even more so when Clive Lloyd led out the local team.

I had been right – Clive and his team were giants. It was amazing to finally see the man I had heard so much about on the radio. Here he was in the flesh and he lived up to all my expectations. He was a big and strong man who oozed confidence. I sat up in the tree for a couple of hours viewing the morning session before I went home, every branch occupied with people as eager as myself to watch the action. It was an unforgettable experience; I had spent a couple of hours amongst gods.

Seeing cricket live made me love the game even more and as a result I played it more often. Unfortunately, I was not good enough to make my school's team and when I went to watch them play, I could see why. All the players were much better than I was. That didn't bother me, because all I wanted to do was play, however and wherever I could.

In 1976, my mother had joined my father in England. I was supposed to follow in a couple of months, but a couple of months turned into a couple of years. I was at home with my gran, so it didn't really make any difference to me. Nevertheless, there was never any doubt that I was still going to England – 'Of course, you are going to England, your mum and dad are there,' I was told. I was having a very happy time in Guyana, surrounded by people who cared for me. It was something I was going to miss.

Eventually my time came. Uncle Wilfred helped me prepare for my adventure and he made me a wicked two-piece suit to wear for the journey. It was bright blue and I felt like a million dollars in it – by then I had grown my own Afro.

Strangely enough, there was no sadness as I got ready to leave, even though I was saying goodbye to and leaving behind those who had brought me up. These were the people who had cared for me and loved me. I think it was because moving to England felt like a normal transition, something all of us aspired to do. I'd seen it a dozen times before, with so many people in our community already choosing this path.

All the stories we had ever heard were positive ones, even the people back home never talked negatively about missing any of their friends or relatives who had gone before. The move to this wonderful new, foreign land was all about grasping opportunities, and families would get together and group what money they had in order to send one of their children to England, to give them a better chance in life. Such a chance was the best thing on offer for many Guyanese.

I was so excited when I saw a jumbo jet for the first time – I couldn't believe that such a big plane could fly. England seemed to be the grandest place imaginable. What an adventure this was going to be, the start of a new and thrilling life. It might seem strange to people now, a 10-year-old boy travelling alone from one part of the world to another, but I had no fears or worries. All kids of my age were very capable and my world seemed to have no dangers in it. I just couldn't wait to get to the mother country to see those streets made of gold.

Looking back at it now, I understand that my grandmother, uncles and aunts would all have been choked when I boarded that flying beast, but they didn't show it. If there were tears, they would have flowed after I left. On the plane, it seemed as if I had already entered into the new world. I had a lot to learn.

I always remember the seatbelts being fastened, cigarettes extinguished and this odd plastic thing pushed up to the back of the seat in front of me.

4

MY DEVELOPING CAREER AS A BOY IN ENGLAND

Growing into my new life began in earnest once I went to my first English school, just a few months after arriving in the country. It was called John Keble, in Harlesden, and it opened a whole new world for me. I realised very quickly that I acted differently and looked different to the other children. I didn't talk like them; I didn't think like them; I didn't behave like them. I had a massive Afro, and from the size of my lips it was unmistakable where I had come from – plus, of course, I liked cricket rather than football. I was not part of any group, so I spent a fair amount of time on my own. None of this felt any different from when I was back home. Both there and in England I made a lot of my own entertainment and I had no problem with that.

One of the first things I discovered in the first term after my arrival was they played cricket at school. This was going to be my time. This was primary school and so, although there was a cricket team, which I very quickly joined, there were only a handful of matches. But in these games I saw a different world. Whereas before, back in Guyana, I didn't seem to be that good, here I seemed a lot more capable. For the first time in my life, I got my hands on a proper cricket bat, gloves, pads and all the other school equipment. Some of the other kids were frightened of the ball hitting them, but not me; I was used to that. The hard ball was not an issue for me and, if anything, it went further when I hit it. It would make a lovely crunching sound, which I loved to hear.

During the three games we played in that summer of 1978, I batted three times and I didn't lose my wicket. Everything was good in my world – or at least in the world of the 'young Gordon Greenidge'. After school, I would race home and play cricket in the back garden. I would bounce a tennis ball off the wall and by the time it came back to where I was standing I was ready, bat in hand, to hit it. I spent many days, weeks, months and indeed years doing this in the garden. I remember I once broke Gary Sobers' record of 365 – I counted every run I made.

I was soon on the move again to a secondary school, Willesden High, aged 11. Even in the winter months, I would carry my bat to school and play whenever I could. Then, the summer term approached. At the first opportunity, I tried to join the cricket team, but was told that I had to go to trials and that my style of bowling – underarm – was not allowed. I had to learn to bowl properly, something I had never done before. Back on the streets of Georgetown I had only ever wanted to bat and would just gently chuck underarm deliveries and wait for the batsman to hit it in the air, to be caught out, so I could grab the bat again.

But now I decided that I had better learn to bowl. If I could do that then I would stand a much better chance of getting into the school team.

I knew the basics – about bringing my right arm close to my ear when delivering – but that was about it. I started with that, trying to keep the seam on the ball upright, something I had heard all the time when listening to the commentary on the radio, and I slowly began to bring my arm over.

In just a couple of days of practice, I taught myself to bowl at a very basic, medium pace. That was at least enough for me to go for a trial for the school team. When I got there, I was nervous. I batted nicely, seeing the ball well, and none of the bowlers I faced concerned me. Then I had a bowl and I kept on hitting the seam. I could bowl as well as bat! The day could not have gone much better.

The PE teacher for the first-year students, Mr Ellis Williams – a man who was to play a huge role over the next few years – told me that I had made the team. Wow! I was elated. I could now look forward to doing what I loved more than anything else – playing cricket, and in a proper team.

I enjoyed being with Mr Williams, a rugby-playing man from Wales. He was to have an impact on my early cricket career. He had time for me and the other members of the team; all of us were taken under his wing. Most important of all, he loved his job and was obviously excited about organising the cricket for our year.

Cricket was an out-of-school activity, which meant that a teacher had to give up their Saturdays. Mr Williams was more than happy to give up his time for us. He was always there for me and we got on very well. I was quiet – due to the way I had been brought up, my family believing that children should only speak when spoken to – and I think that he liked that about me. At lunchtimes at school, Mr Williams would let me have the keys to the gymnasium so I could play games with my friends. There were lots of games to choose from, but a friend of mine, Dipen Patel, and I pretty much always chose cricket.

I owe Mr Williams so much for allowing me to develop my game, giving me both his time and his trust. Later, on many occasions, he watched me play in Test matches and I was thrilled to have him there. He seemed to take an awful lot of pride in my performance. After being released from jail, I spoke to him and we arranged to meet up, but I then received a call informing me that he had died.

It would have been lovely to see him again. I would like to say to him now, 'Rest well, you did your job superbly and you made a big difference to the life of at least one person. I thank you from the bottom of my heart. You were a wonderful human being.'

I travelled to Llanelli for his funeral at the start of January 2016. Everybody there echoed my thoughts about Mr Williams; so many talked about how he had touched their lives, including some fellow former teachers from Willesden High. It was a nostalgic and humbling day. I felt like a little boy again.

I was lucky to have gone to Willesden High. Another teacher, Godfrey Evans, the head of PE, was a real cricket man and made sure that sport was arranged throughout the school for those who wanted to play it. A few years later, when myself and Phil DeFreitas (who also went to Willesden High) were representing England in Australia, we saw Mr Evans and we asked him what he was doing there. He said that he had some time off so he

CRAZY: MY ROAD TO REDEMPTION

thought he would come and watch us play – such was the passion and feeling Mr Evans and Mr Williams had for their jobs and, more importantly, the people they encountered. Luther Blissett, Dave Beasant and a host of others were products of Mr Evans in that period. Unsurprisingly, we won a lot of trophies, and thanks to Mr Evans and Mr Williams a number of pupils went on to achieve their dreams. I really can't speak highly enough of these men. It's hard to put into words the affect they had on me at a very important time of my life. They both made sure that the facilities were there for me when I needed them and they were always there with encouragement and support.

On the morning of my very first game for the school team, Mr Williams told me that it was between a friend, Ian Ervine, and I as to who was to be named as captain. This was a bolt from the blue. I was happy just to have scraped into the team but now to be told I could be captain, I was amazed and astonished. This was great stuff for an 11-year-old and hard for me to take in. I could never have imagined it.

I had sometimes thought that, since arriving in London, I was no good at anything. This was because I had only recently arrived in the capital. I didn't fully grasp or understand most of the conversations that other children were having. I would listen, but was never able to contribute much to any of the group discussions because, more often than not, I didn't know what they were talking about. Now, here was something that I felt at home with, a sport that, according to Mr Williams at any rate, I was good at. Cricket made me stand out proudly – it was my thing.

I became the captain of the team and it was then that, for the first time, I got to be a proper cricketer. The few games

I had played at primary school were on artificial pitches, but here I was playing on a grass pitch. This is how I had always imagined it. I batted with my floppy hat, like the great West Indian batsmen of the time, and I opened the batting, just like Gordon. In our 20 overs, we scored 80 or 90 and I had made 65 of them. Yes! This was it! This was how I was going to enjoy every Saturday for the rest of the summer. This was the best I had ever felt in my life. I had the whites on, all the gear – my pads, gloves, boots, everything.

Once I had made the team, my mum and dad got me all I needed. But, as with a lot of immigrants from the Caribbean, the grown-ups were obsessed with their kids becoming doctors or accountants – good, honest professions that had some form of status symbol attached to them (years later, mum would still pull a face when introducing me to people with, 'This is my son, the cricketer'), although at this time they were very happy that I had found something I enjoyed doing.

That Saturday afternoon in the early part of the summer of 1979, perhaps for the first time, I thought that I was all right at this game of cricket. I had played pull shots, hooks, cuts – all the shots – and hadn't done badly at all. It was perfect, played on a beautiful early summer's day at a nice ground. This was everything I had dreamt of, and a lot more besides.

Then I discovered that there was cricket on the TV on Sundays – the John Player League. My first memory was of watching David Gower playing for Leicestershire. He could bat and looked so classy, the more I stared at the TV the more my imagination was caught. I wanted to be a cricketer, I wanted to be the next David Gower. He moved like a West Indian without trying. He was so graceful when he was batting.

Of course, all my previous heroes were from the West Indian team, but now Gower was amongst them, as was Ian Botham. I remember listening to Botham's debut for England at Trent Bridge in 1977 on the radio at home. He was the most exciting cricketer I had ever come across on that radio. People batted and bowled, of course, but Ian Botham did everything, seemingly playing a shot every other ball. 'Ah, it's another square cut from Botham,' the commentators would purr. They seemed to be so excited about him, and as a boy who learned so much from that radio, I became excited too.

England was not so bad after all. There were major differences between my old life and my new one, though. I was growing during my time at Willesden High and I developed an important friendship with a young boy named Dipen Patel. His family was from Uganda and they had arrived in England after leaving the Idi Amin-led country. Like me, Dipen had a passion for the sport of cricket and we got to know each other well through the game. As players, we stood out from the rest. We were the only ones who took our bats to school and we played cricket as much as we could.

For a long time I had played by myself in the garden at home after the school day had finished, but now I had someone else to play with. The two of us would often go to the adventure playground, which was just a couple of doors away from my aunt's house. It had lots of apparatus and a brick walkway, about a dozen yards long, which we decided to use as our cricket pitch. The two of us spent hour after hour developing our skills, although we didn't know that's what we were doing at the time. Every day after school we would play cricket. We lived for cricket and played at every opportunity. We had to run around a tree in order to bowl, but one day a man from the council spoke to us in the park and asked us about changes we would like to see in the playground. We said we would like the tree to be moved so we could run in properly, and the following week it was gone.

One Christmas Day, while our families were preparing for the festivities, we went out to play, but it had been snowing, so we swept the snow away and played anyway, such was our desire to play the game. Dipen and I would use something called a 'pudding ball', which was a really hard rubber ball. I remember, even now, how much the ball would sting if you were hit on the leg with it. We didn't use pads, which meant that the two of us had to keep our eyes on the ball and to play it with the bat as much as possible.

Over time, a friend called Jim Dallan who lived across the road would join us, as did Ken Blake, another friend of mine who bowled just like Mike Proctor, his arms all over the place but delivering with pace, especially from the short distance of our makeshift pitch. Dipen, meanwhile, was fast. He was strong for an 11-year-old and was bowling probably as quickly as anyone of his age in the county at that time. We would make the most of the winter months, but in truth we all wanted each summer to come around as quickly as possible, so we could be out on the grass playing real games against other schools.

At the same time, my brother's dad, Bill, who captained the Post Office cricket team, invited me to play for them on Sundays, mainly because they were short of players. So, my weekends were now filled with doing just what I wanted to do. We played mostly against West Indian teams, and that helped me to feel more at home in my new environment. The players from both sides would bring their families and food, and hearing everyone talk in the language I had grown up with reminded me of being back home in the Caribbean. Cricket was no longer just a game I loved being involved in, it was also a reminder of where I had come from.

There was often a carnival atmosphere with a lot of chatter and noise out on the field. I remember one game when I was batting quite well – playing some nice shots for a young boy – and the wife of the bowler was giving him a hard time for being hit for four by an 11-year-old. 'Lick him down!' she kept shouting. 'Bounce him out!' He tried, but I held my corner, much to the amusement of many at the ground, probably with the exception of the wife. But there was also a lot of love towards me during these games.

At another match, I batted for the last half an hour and we won the game. After the game had finished, the opposing captain and his team stayed on the field to give me some more practice, how good was that?

I was having a great time. So great, in fact, that I really didn't want to do anything else except play cricket. I would play all day, then go home, put my gear back on and play in my bedroom for half the night. Cricket dominated pretty much every thought as I moved into my teenage years.

I loved playing for the school, and with Dipen and I doing well, along with Ian Ervine and some other good players, we became a formidable team. We rarely lost a game over several years together, but as far as I was concerned there just weren't enough matches for my liking. We played only about half a dozen games throughout a summer and so I decided that I needed to join a local cricket club – I needed to play more.

Dipen felt the same way, and so off we went to South Hampstead. We walked up to the ground and peeked through the wooden fence. We could hardly believe our eyes – the cricket club was immaculate, it looked to us just how we'd imagined a Test match ground to be. We'd never seen anything quite like it; the grass and the pavilion shone out to the two of us and we were in awe of what we were seeing. This was it, this was the club we both wanted to play for and we wanted to do that as soon as possible.

We were soon part of the South Hampstead Colts section and at the age of 14, for the very first time I was part of a cricket club. It's funny looking back now, but until this time, strange as it may seem, I had never been part of a club of any kind before. So, what went on with secret handshakes or secret bonds I had no clue about. I was just excited to be able to play cricket. Of course, not knowing what was expected of me would cause problems later, but for now Dipen and I were in cricket heaven. It wasn't too long before we were asked to play for the Third XI; again, largely because they were often short of players. Did we want to play? Of course, we did!

By the age of 15, I was selected for a Brent school (an area in north-west London) trip to tour Trinidad and Tobago. My mum and aunt took me to the trials, but I was at that age when I didn't want them to come into the ground – I didn't want anyone to think that I still needed my parents to take me to cricket. I performed well and made the team, and for the first time since coming to England I was off back to the Caribbean – to Trinidad and Tobago, not a million miles from where I was raised.

The tour was managed by Dick Porter, a teacher from a local school, Alperton High. I had met Dick many times while playing against his school and he was a man I liked. He organised lots of sports for young people in Brent and was always very encouraging. I was told through a letter in the post that I had been successful and was selected for the tour. My mum and aunt paid for the trip.

I was heading back to the Caribbean. There, each of the players was billeted out to stay with a local family. It's funny sometimes how things work out. Thirty years later my phone rings: 'Chris, it's Bobby, how you doing man?' Bobby was the head of the family I had stayed with all those years ago in Trinidad, I had not spoken to him since I was 15. We were all treated beautifully by some very gracious people and had a wonderful time. I had been selected as a batsman, but with several people enjoying the local sunshine a little too much and coming down with sunstroke, I was asked to open the bowling. I felt this was a bit of a chore, but with reluctantly accepted and got the ball to swing, ending up taking 21 wickets and coming back as the leading wicket-taker of the team. I was batting well, but without ever making a big score. I always felt good at the crease but would get myself out, I just couldn't leave it outside that off stump.

While I was resting for one of the matches I sat, hidden from view, watching my team. I overheard Mr Porter talking to a group of people, running through the players on the tour and saying who might make it as professional cricketers. When he got to my name, my ears pricked up. I was ready to be hailed as one who had a great future in the game; instead, Mr Porter said that I would make a good club cricketer but not a county one. I was disappointed. I hadn't decided at that time of my life that I wanted to play cricket professionally, I hadn't dared to dream of such a thing, but I wasn't sure of what else I would do either. Hearing Mr Porter's judgement on my abilities saddened me a little bit. I remember the feeling even today, but my reaction soon became, 'Well, how does he possibly know what my future holds?' I wasn't angry, but it did somehow help to motivate me – hearing that I was not good enough to be a professional cricketer made me want to become one even more.

It was an odd experience, returning to the Caribbean. Playing there brought back all sorts of childhood memories – the familiarity of the people and their love of cricket. They treated me as one of their own, as they would do years later when I played for England. It was natural that I felt so comfortable here; it had, after all, been my home.

One of the other grown-ups on the tour was a man called John Haskell, who was, and still is, a member of Wembley Cricket Club. He liked what he had seen in me and asked me to join his club. I made the move on my return to England and was included in their second team.

Wembley also put me forward for the Middlesex County Colts. At the trial, I batted for twenty minutes and made 3 runs but, crucially, I didn't get out. I was determined to show them that I could bat, and I wanted to prove that I could bat correctly. I thought I had done well, but at the same trials there was a 13-year-old boy who looked absolute class, right from the off. He was younger than the rest of us, but that didn't make any difference to him – he stood out.

The rest of us wondered who this wonder kid was. I asked around and nobody had heard of him or played against him anywhere. He batted for a while without getting out, looking ever so correct in everything he did. Finally, I was told his name.

He was a young man who was to go on and score more than 100 first-class centuries, and within a few years he was to make an immediate impact for Middlesex in a one-day cup final at Lord's. His name was Mark Ramprakash.

I thought I had done okay at the trials, and I clearly did enough to impress, as I was soon told via a letter that I had made the team – as a batsman. I didn't bowl at the trial, and at this point in my life I was barely bowling medium pace, so I didn't consider myself to be a bowler yet. I would take wickets by hitting the seam and nipping the ball around, but I didn't think too much about the art of bowling. It was just one of those things I did from time to time to help my team.

By the end of the summer of 1984, I was asked to play in a first-team game for Wembley. The opposition had a player who just didn't look like a sportsman; he looked as if he had just fallen out of a pub. Out he came to bat and he smashed the ball to all parts of the field, me included. It was clear to me why he was able to do this. He may not have looked like much of a cricketer, but he had a good eye and he took me on due to my pace, or rather lack of it. I just wasn't quick enough if the ball wasn't moving. I didn't like this treatment one little bit – it was the first time that I had been battered by a batsman. Of course, I had been hit for fours and sixes before, but nothing like this. Every single ball I delivered seemed to be thumped into the distance.

I didn't want that to happen again, so during the winter I tried to bowl quicker. I realised that previously I had only delivered the ball, putting the ball in the right areas but not trying to bowl quickly. I had an advantage too – I was still growing. That winter in the nets, I wanted to see if I could bowl with pace – running in, hitting the crease, straining my body. I can remember my first victim, a Wembley teammate called Chris Ede. I bowled a bouncer and Chris hardly got out of his stance before the ball was on him. The atmosphere around the nets changed in an instant; suddenly, people didn't want to face me.

The new season arrived and I was back at Wembley with renewed confidence. I played for the club on both Saturdays and Sundays, and tried to get in as many midweek games as I could as well. The big change was that people started to see me more as a bowler. This was not how I had planned things; after all, I was going to be the next Gordon Greenidge. Now though, the captains I played under kept giving me the ball and I was bowling with little bit more aggression. I was getting stronger, and the more I bowled the stronger I became, but fast bowling is not all about strength. My timing was coming together and my rhythm improved. I felt like I was putting in the same amount of effort as in previous years, but now the ball was coming out of my hand a lot quicker than before. I was hitting batsmen's gloves and making them uncomfortable.

Towards the end of that season, Wembley was playing a game against Winchmore Hill, a good side with several contracted Middlesex players within their ranks. I bowled well in the match and took 5 for 50, but the thing I remember the most was that some of the batsmen were backing away when I bowled, not the contracted players. I knew I had put on pace but I had never imagined that it was the sort of pace that put the frighteners on the opposing batsmen. Don Wilson, Middlesex's second-team coach, was watching the game, and I must have impressed him enough because he asked me to play in a Middlesex Under-25 match against Leicestershire in the one-day competition, as the county was often short of players. I played twice and both games were against Leicestershire. In the first of them, I had bowled my medium pace, just trying to make sure that I hit the seam, and the Leicestershire batsmen did the rest, hitting the ball to hand to give me figures of 4 for 24.

My batting was less of a success. I had never come across the speed of George Ferris, who was in the Leicestershire Second XI and bowling rapidly. I had heard of George. I had been in the country long enough at this stage of my life, and had followed cricket so religiously, watching it and reading magazines, that I knew a lot about the players on the professional circuit. George's was often spoken about.

I was never unduly worried about facing pace or moving up to new levels of the sport. As a batsman nothing really fazed me, as I would always adopt the same approach. To me it was quite simple, the method was always the same – you watch the ball. If you think the bowler will deliver at 1,000mph and you think you can't possibly play it, the process is exactly the same. You can scare yourself by thinking, 'Ah, this guy is bigger than me, he is a couple of years older than me, he can bowl quicker than anything I've ever faced before,' but all you need to do is watch the ball and then deal with it as you've always done, forgetting any inferiority complex you might have.

This would hold me in good stead when I was signed by Leicestershire as an 18-year-old. As I recall, I had a call from Phillip DeFreitas, who had played in the same Willesden High team as myself, even though he was a couple of years older (we would later become the first two players from the same school to open the bowling for England). I was told of Leicestershire's interest in me and I was invited to head north to take part in some trial matches. But Middlesex was my county and I was starting to make strides through their system. I had never thought that if I was lucky enough to take up this brilliant game as a career it would be with any other county than Middlesex. I had played for their Colts, lived in the county and desperately wanted to represent them; that's where I wanted to be. So I declined the offer of having a trial for Leicestershire.

Later that summer there was another call, but this time it was not offering me the opportunity of a trial. Instead, would you believe it, the carrot being dangled in front of me was a two-year contract. In the second of my matches for Middlesex Under-25s against Leicestershire, I had taken 2 for 30-odd, and one of the guys I bowled to was Tim Boon. Tim had told Ken Higgs, the coach at Grace Road, that he should sign me right away, largely, as I understood it, because of a couple of deliveries I had bowled to Tim – one that moved away and one that had jagged back at him. For Tim, that showed that I had a lot of skill and control, but for me it simply meant that I had hit the seam.

This all seemed to be very odd. I was being offered a contract for my bowling, something I had only ever tried overarm just half a dozen years before. A two-year professional contract? Now, this was something that really pricked my ears up. Well, I jumped at the chance. I was hoping to be a paid cricketer one day, but I had no idea if or when that might happen; maybe next year, or maybe five years down the line. Now, right here, was the chance to fulfil my dream. I could hardly believe it. Just a couple of years before, I had been playing Third XI cricket for South Hampstead and now here I was being offered my dream job.

I went off to Middlesex to chat to their chief executive. He told me that my home county would also offer me a one-year deal, but only if I could prove my fitness – I had played in a Second XI fixture for Middlesex against Surrey that had not gone well. I didn't have any bowling boots, as I still didn't consider myself to be much of a bowler. I had no knowledge of bowling really, knowing nothing about the amount of weight going through your feet in the delivery stride. Most of the time my feet seemed to take care of me and I would just bowl. But now, in this game, effectively bowling in plimsolls, I injured my back – the first injury I had encountered from overstraining.

I thought that Middlesex's offer was a little odd – if they were aware of my lack of fitness, why would they be offering me a contract based on that fitness? That made my eventual decision an easy one. I was going to Leicester to become a professional cricketer. I was ecstatic, overjoyed; I had been a child until now, living with my Aunt Hazel, but suddenly I was going to be moving away from my family and I was tingling with excitement at the prospect.

But during all of this there was an interesting thought running through my head, it was about my little brother, Mark. He was only 4 years old. I remember going into hospital as a young boy, just a couple of hours after he was born. I was soon picking him up, a youngster with no cares in the world, thrilled to be holding a baby brother. When I picked him up for the first time, the whole world seemed to stop. I was hit by the most amazing emotional feeling and when I looked at him in my arms, in that moment our relationship was formed. It was the first time that the word 'love' had meant anything to me. I felt it. Now I knew what others meant when they said it. This little boy was all new, and when I looked at him I was filled with something that I had never experienced before. I had to put Mark down, I thought I would drop him, the emotion was so overpowering.

Four years on, and amongst all the celebrations of being offered a chance to fulfil my dream with Leicestershire, Mark asked his older brother if he was going away. It dawned on me that I hadn't thought about Mark since taking the call from Grace Road. I had hardly spent a day apart from him since he was born. I would carry him around, taking him to so many places, and now here he was with a very difficult question: 'Chris, are you going away?' Then it hit me. If I were to go, I would be saying goodbye to him, leaving him behind. I loved him, and I knew that he loved me, so how could I do this? He had become part of my cricket matches in the garden. I had taught him how to play the cover drive and how to bowl, as well as teaching him to play basketball and tennis at the local sports centre, having so much fun together. But now, amongst the euphoria, I felt as if I was about to abandon him. It was tough. Leaving him behind and not being able to play the part in his life I wanted to play was the most difficult decision I'd had to make at this point in life.

But I could not turn down this dream job and I worked out that, initially, I would be able to return home at weekends, and when I did I was always delighted when I saw Mark's little face at the window. When he spotted me, his eyes would light up. It was the most warming sight and an awesome feeling, one I always looked forward to. But here I was, about to leave home and branch out, playing cricket. Perfect.

5

THE RISE AND RISE

I was on my way to Leicester. I went up the M1 a few times to meet Ken Higgs and the CEO of the county club, Mike Turner, to discuss my contract. There wasn't really too much to talk about, however, as I just wanted to play cricket. I think my first salary was £3,000 for the six-month contract, in those days only lasting for the summer months, but I was happy with that. It was £3,000 more than I was currently being paid and I was going to be a professional cricketer.

Once at Leicester, the idea of being on the same team as David Gower, Peter Willey, Jonathan Agnew, Paddy Clift or Les Taylor did not seem to match up. Gower was a once-in-a-generation batsman and the same could be said of the hard-as-nails Willey. I had watched them both on the TV as a young man and I admired them enormously for different reasons. As a batsman, Gower was so pretty and elegant, while Willey was more of a man's man, one who seemed impossible to scare and a player who would gut it out when the going seemed to get impossibly tough.

Was I ready for this? I didn't think so. Of course, I didn't verbalise that to anyone and I was very thankful that I was a professional cricketer now, but, boy, how was I going to do this? I had the confidence but now I really had to prove myself to my new teammates.

To begin with, I didn't really hang out too much with those aforementioned Leicestershire big guns. I was a second-team player, although not for too long. I remember the first pre-season fixtures coming out and both Lloyd Tennant (a young and talented right-arm swing bowler) and myself were included in this First XI fixture. The younger lads had a bet on which one of us would go for the most runs and they all bet on me. I would probably have done the same thing, but the reality was that in a match against Northamptonshire I was able to bowl reasonably well. I got the ball to move about and I wasn't hit to the boundary too often. I ended up with a fairly cheap 3-wicket haul. It was not a bad introduction, especially given the sleepless nights I'd had thinking about playing against first-class opposition. I had a lot to prove and, although I wasn't always sure why the batsmen didn't go after me, I was very pleased with the way things had turned out.

Once I'd arrived at Leicester, the club arranged for me to stay with George Ferris and Winston Benjamin, two very different characters also from the Caribbean, but both very good company. I couldn't believe my luck. It meant that I was going to enjoy some good Caribbean food and good music. George and Winston were happy to share some advice as well.

George had a bit of a reputation for hitting people with cricket balls. He was genuinely the first professional fast bowler I had seen up close and personal. As our friendship grew, I witnessed the effort that George put in to generate the pace that he got off the wicket. He didn't sprint in, but rather started with a jog that turned into something else, a bit like a javelin thrower's build up, Then, there was this explosion as he got into his delivery stride. I watched him with amazement, wondering how on earth he could get the ball to carry so far. He was ferociously fast at times, a real handful for most batsmen. Yet off the field he was a gentleman.

In our house share, George was always singing, especially songs by Jeffrey 'The Voice' Osborne, as George would call him, and Earth, Wind & Fire (or, according to George, 'Ert, Wind & Fire' – but who was I to tell him any different, I was still saying 'flim' instead of 'film'). George would belt out their tunes; he had a good voice to go with it. But with a ball in his hand, he was a very different character. He wasn't mean but was always up for business and he was in the business of taking wickets and putting the frighteners on opposing batsmen. Winston ('Benjy') on the other hand hardly ever smiled, and definitely not on demand. Benjy did Benjy, which meant that he was sometimes misunderstood. He was seen as moody and sulky by some, but they were just labels given to him by those who didn't take the time to get to know him. He was an athlete. He ran to the crease in an easy and relaxed manner and delivered the ball with real quality.

Living with the two of them certainly helped me to settle in, and in this new environment gave me permission to be more myself, both of them teaching me the ropes as I learned the life of a professional cricketer. When I was not at the ground, I spent most of my time at home with these two guys. Spending time with them on and off the field opened my eyes and I thank them for making me feel at home. After the day was done, we didn't focus our conversation on cricket unless we were talking specifically about something or were giving constructive criticism; instead we would put our energy into other things. We watched TV and joked with each other, with George being the man in charge in the kitchen. Sometimes I couldn't wait for the pot to stop boiling and for the dumplings, plantain and cassava to be brought out. It was a home away from home.

That first pre-season was an eye-opener. The limited training I'd had before in club cricket generally consisted of going to nets in the evening, batting for ten minutes if I was lucky and then bowling for an hour. This was just once or twice a week. At Leicester, we worked for three or four hours each morning, had a break and then trained for the same amount of time in the afternoon. I was in my element, although it was tiring. By the end of the first week I was shattered, my muscles had been given a real workout. We had to run down the side of the canal as well as doing lots of practice, all of this at the start of spring when it was cold and wet more often than not; it took some getting used to.

In the following years, I always ensured that I trained to get ready for pre-season so I didn't have to start from scratch. The first mornings back after a winter off were always the toughest and people did well not to throw up. The training lasted about a month and then we were ready to go. Physically it was tough, while mentally I was just amazed to actually be doing this – a professional cricketer in England. I knew I could play cricket,

I'd known that since I was a kid, but only a few months before this I'd been playing club cricket for Wembley. At times I had to pinch myself. Was this really happening? I was in the same environment as Gower, Willey, DeFreitas, who was now in the England side, and James Whitaker. I sometimes wondered if the county had made a mistake, until I got to play my first game.

The 1987 season was properly underway and I was with the second team playing for the first time against Glamorgan. I was disappointed when I saw the batting order: I was in at number ten. Paddy Clift, a Zimbabwean cricketer, whom I was fortunate enough to spend the very early part of my career with, came over to me and said that I should bat in front of him, so we swapped places. It was a lovely gesture on Paddy's behalf. I got 60 runs – a big relief. Not only did I score the runs but I also played an innings in the way I wanted to, and it turned out to be good enough for the company I was in. I had made a start to my professional life and immediately ticked a box. When it was my turn to bowl, I let the ball go with some pace and aggression, taking 6 wickets in the match. At times, I appeared to be a handful for the batsmen, but I must admit again that I didn't always know what I was doing when bowling. That game was a watershed for me. Afterwards, I knew that I was good enough. It was my first match and I had taken wickets and scored runs. It felt great.

For the rest of the summer I trained during the day and really enjoyed playing our second-team matches and hanging out at the ground with the likes of Justin Benson, Alan Mullally, Paul Nixon and co. We were young men living the dream and having fun, showing off to one another and proving to the others that we could catch, run, bat, bowl; that we could do absolutely anything we wanted. Ken Higgs was our coach and at times he must have been pulling his hair out.

In matches, Justin and I would have bets about who could hit the first ball we faced out of the ground. I would come charging down the wicket and spoon the ball just over the mid-on's head. The guys would love it, but Ken would be doing his nut. They were fun times, for sure. We didn't think that we were invincible, but we did think we could play every shot in the book and, perhaps because of that, things progressed quickly. At the age of 18, Ken had the confidence to put me in the first team. Just a year before, I had been playing club cricket for Wembley and now here I was, loving life, loving the game and proving that I could play it.

On 6 June 1987, I was selected to make my first-class debut for a match at home to Worcestershire. As I was not part of the initial squad, I had decided to take the opportunity to head back to London to see my family. On the way, I popped in to the ground to watch Graeme Hick, as I had never seen him play before. While I was there, I was told that Winston Benjamin was not fit to play and, as there was no one else available, they asked me to take his place. It rained for much of the game and coming in at number 8 I was out for a duck. But, with a ball in hand, I bagged two scalps: those of future England batsman Tim Curtis, who was caught by Nigel Briers in the covers, my first championship wicket, and then Martin Weston, who I bowled for nought. One nipped in and one nipped away. I ended with figures of 2 for 40 from 15 overs. I even bowled to Hick, a batsman who was not only the talk of the town back then but the whole cricketing world. He had, for a while, been scoring runs for fun. I would look at Teletext and just see his runs adding up, one huge score after another, with double hundreds, triple hundreds and even a quadruple one. When I bowled to him he hit one so hard that the ball bounced back off the boundary boards and almost back onto the square.

Later in my career, I was fortunate to play in the same England team as Hick. He was an exceptional player, although once he started playing for England he did not have it easy and, in some ways, he faced the same charge as me for not fulfilling his potential, alongside Mark Ramprakash. The expectations on Hick were enormous but I admired him for his approach. He just got on with playing cricket.

I had enjoyed every minute of my debut. Overall, I played four first-class matches in my first summer, scoring 53 runs with a top score of 42, while taking 5 wickets with a best of 2 for 26.

But my first real taste of a big crowd was a NatWest Trophy semi-final at Grace Road against our neighbours, Northamptonshire. It was the largest crowd I had ever played in front of, it made me tingle. Until then, I didn't realise that I liked playing in front of an audience, I hadn't thought about it before. Alas, it was another match that was affected by the weather and Leicestershire lost heavily, but I remember being very excited with my efforts – 1 for 47 from my 11 overs and 15 runs – batting at number 9.

My cricket was on the up as I learnt from those around me. I quickly became aware of the importance of my first county coach, Ken Higgs. He was a fantastic man. He and his wife Mary really looked after me and we had a wonderful relationship. He was nothing short of a phenomenon. Ken saw something in me that he thought was worth pursuing. He saw me in the nets practising at Lord's and spoke to the coaches there to find out more about me. He then brought me to Leicester and offered me a two-year contract without a trial game. Just weeks after arriving at Grace Road, Ken came to me and told me that one day I would play for England; of course I didn't believe him, so Ken made a bet: 'I bet you half of your first Test match fee that you'll play.' I made that bet, I couldn't lose. Ken won. I went to see Ken and Mary, money in hand, but they told me that I should put it in the bank and take care of my money.

Ken was the man who really taught me about the craft of bowling and about what I was doing with the ball. He was responsible for securing my first sponsored car. Ken was, quite simply, the man and I can't stress that enough. Half an hour in his presence on the field and he had me bowling just right and feeling great. It might have been just the smallest adjustment, but he always got it spot on. He was a genius.

I want to use this opportunity to say a huge thank you to him and Mary, who sadly is no longer with us. The two of them were my parents away from home. As a young man in Leicester, the two were gracious and loving towards me and I owe them both so much. Ken lived by the ground at Grace Road and would come over in his spare time to bowl at me in the nets or to show me what to do. I don't think that I would have ever gone from being somebody who perhaps had a bit of ability, to a first-class cricketer, and one good enough to eventually play for England without him. During the latter stages of writing this book, I received the news that Ken had passed away at the age of 79. I attended his funeral, principally because of the impact he had on my career and our friendship. I was pleased to see some of my old teammates there, but I was disappointed that there was not a larger turnout. Ken was a man who inspired so many of the people he played with and coached. Of course, as well as being a hell of a bowler, he is well known still at Grace Road for producing Leicestershire's best last-wicket partnership of 228 with Ray Illingworth against Northamptonshire in 1977, in which he hit a career best of 98. Incredibly, the season before my debut, he made his last appearance for Leicestershire at the age of 49, making an emergency return to the team for a match against Yorkshire in which he took 5 for 22. That statistic alone emphasises what an incredible man Ken Higgs was. I will always remember him.

My first captain, Peter Willey, was a no-nonsense type of guy and he rubbed some people up the wrong way, but never me. Peter was always to the point and direct, a hard taskmaster. I was having the time of my life by being able to observe the likes of Peter up close and personal. I liked him, and I liked the way he played his cricket, too. If you have the ability to front-up, as he so often did, any sportsman should admire such a man. Peter hit the ball as hard as he was, and I am so happy now to see his son, David, doing so well in the sport with England. In addition, Peter was a very fine umpire. He was a man who had the kind of stature in the game that made him always worth listening to.

David Gower was among the biggest names in English cricket. It was interesting watching David play. Everyone was exhausted running around at 100mph. David, however, appeared chilled. My approach was similar to his. I preferred relaxing, listening to some music and chilling out in readiness for the match. David and I were hardly peas in a pod – I can't imagine music was his gig before a match – but he showed me that you could be chilled and still play this game, that there was more than one way to skin a cat when it came to preparation. Being around such players at the start of my professional career influenced me greatly. If I could have bottled the calm and relaxed nature of Gower and the up-for-a-fight gutsy nature of Willey and put them together, I would have been the ideal cricketer.

At the end of season one, Ken Higgs informed me that I'd been picked for England Young Cricketers to go to the Youth World Cup in Australia. I wasn't aware of that competition but this would be an unbelievable honour. I had imagined that I would have come back down to earth in the winter with no cricket to play, but now I had more of a purpose. This was good news indeed and I was overjoyed. I was on a real high but, in truth, I couldn't fully understand why I had been picked. There was a huge amount of improvement needed in my game – I was still learning. It was challenging to be competing with the skilled performers in county cricket; nevertheless, this was an honour. I travelled to London to tell my family the news, who were as thrilled and excited as I was, although I don't think my mum and aunt knew what I was talking about. I also informed them that Leicestershire had increased my pay based on my first-year performances. I was now up to the dizzy heights of £5,000 for the summer.

The team I travelled to Australia with were quite something. Opening the batting in the 50-over tournament was Mark Ramprakash, the young boy I had seen with Middlesex as a 13-year-old. I had come across him a few times since then and he always impressed. At that age, Ramps was the best young batsman that I had ever seen in my life. It's almost impossible to describe how good he was at such a young age. He looked like a miniature Viv Richards with his SS Jumbo bat and an attitude and confidence at the crease that matched. Surely he was going to be a world beater; he was streets ahead of anyone else for his age. There was also Trevor Ward, Nasser Hussain, Mark Alleyne, Martin Bicknell, Simon Brown, Warren Hegg and Peter Martin, amongst others, including the captain Michael Atherton.

Michael was a good captain. In a match against New Zealand, I was bowling at one end and the ball was bouncing nicely for me. I was pleased with everything, even though I was going for a few runs. Michael took me off and switched me to the other end where there was not as much bounce. I was not best pleased but importantly I took 3 wickets. Michael knew exactly what he was doing. He was also a real fighter with bat in hand against the new ball, which of course made for the middle and lower-middle orders to have an easier time of it. That was the job of the opener and Michael was exceptional at it. He always showed his steel, which is something I admired enormously about him. I played a lot over the years with Michael and Nasser Hussain, a man who always made me laugh. I can't remember too many serious words being exchanged. When Nasser wanted to, he could have a very sharp tongue, but for me that was part of his charm, he loved a moan. Before a match I would be very quiet, it was my way of approaching a game. Nasser commented on how different my personality was on match days. For me, preparing to play was as much about getting ready mentally as it was physically. Being quiet with my own thoughts was the way I went about achieving this. As usual I was enjoying the whole experience. I loved being in Australia, the place was just stunning. The people were very warm and friendly and I had a great time. Here I was representing England in Australia, with, on paper at least, a team that was capable of winning the competition.

Playing for the young West Indies was one Brian Charles Lara, who I met in Australia for the first time. I soon realised that we had something in common – we both liked to party. We were based in Adelaide, the hottest place I had ever encountered. One night, I went into the city looking for a bit of adventure and went clubbing by myself where I danced the night away. I was in Australia for the first time; I was a young man who loved music and loved dancing. I didn't drink alcohol at the time, so my nights out would generally start much later than everyone else's as I had to wait for the nightclubs to open and fill up. On this night, I was still going at five in the morning and, as the crowd of people thinned out in the club, I spotted Brian on his own doing pretty much the same thing as myself. We had a little chat and then went our separate ways, but that became a theme over the tournament, seeing Brian out in the early hours of the morning. Years later, when touring the Caribbean with England, Brian would show me some of the spots he hung out at in Trinidad.

Despite being with such a talented bunch, many of whom I had previously met on the county circuit, we lost the first game to India. What I remember most was the stifling heat. Every couple of overs, drinks were brought out. It was thirsty work, tough. Our tour was up and down. I hit a 66 in a loss to Australia and took 5 for 39 as we thrashed Pakistan, but overall we underachieved as a team. None of the batsmen really fired, apart from Nasser.

Yet we made it to the semi-finals and met the Aussies again in Adelaide. The hosts included in their team a man who was to play alongside me a lot in the coming years – Alan Mullally. I did not have a good game at all and we didn't perform as a team, losing comfortably. But I'd done well overall and was named as the Player Most Likely to Succeed. I had scored runs, taken wickets and bowled faster than I had ever bowled before.

Back home after the tournament, I was buzzing. I was now looking forward to the next challenge, to try to establish myself in the Leicestershire first team in the summer of 1988. My experience in Australia had undoubtedly made me a more confident player and it was an experience that I knew would help me as I entered the new season back at Leicestershire. I was feeling stronger than ever, my body condition was improving due to all the training and my rhythm and timing got better.

The first game of the new season was a warm-up match with Oxford University at the Parks. I came on first change in the first innings and took 4 for 48, and in the second I managed figures of 6 for 22, which would turn out to be the best of my career.

Thanks to match figures of 10 for 70, I was selected for the opening championship game of the summer at Derby. I was excited because in the previous year I was only picked for the four games played in because of injuries to other players. Finally, I had been chosen not because of injuries to others but on my own merit.

We won the toss and put Derbyshire in to bat. The wicket was green, as they mostly tended to be in April at the start of a new season, and that was exactly what I needed. I came on and bowled my line and length, nibbling the ball away nicely and finding the edge to take some early wickets, 3 in fact, all caught behind the stumps by Phil Whitticase. But then things changed and I kept passing the outside edge. I received some advice from the umpire, Dicky Bird, a man who always made me laugh. 'Get in closer, lad,' he told me, 'and then they will nick it.' He was right. I did just what he said and the batsman did exactly that. I had my first championship five-fer, ending with 5 for 73. I added figures of 1–109 in the second innings. Such is the nature of being a bowler: one day you take a bundle of wickets and the next you go for 100 runs. Nevertheless, I was buoyed by my efforts and I was looking forward to the rest of the championship summer. By the end of 1988, I was established in the first team. I played in fifteen first-class matches, taking 41 wickets and scoring 337 runs.

In the close season, with no cricket to play, I decided to stay in Leicestershire and found lodgings with teammate Phil Whitticase in a little village called Stoney Stanton. I worked at the local post office, sorting and delivering the early morning mail. This was, of course, quite a change, waking up at five in the morning, heading to the sorting office, getting the post ready and then getting on my bike to deliver the letters. The upside of all this was that I was finished by midday and had the rest of the day to myself.

However, delivering the mail in a small Leicestershire village was not without incident. Let's just say I was the only person of colour. There were scrapes with dogs chasing me down the streets and getting my fingers nibbled by them as I attempted to put the post through the letterbox. Those minor scrapes paled into insignificance when one morning the police were called. A young woman, possibly off school for the day, had observed me walking towards her address in an effort to deliver some mail, but I struggled to get the mail through the letterbox. Heaven knows what she must have been thinking, but the police were called. Fortunately, when they arrived and recognised me as the new postman we quickly sorted things out and all had a laugh about it. It was all part of the experience.

Stoney Stanton, like a lot of villages, seemed to be centred around the local pubs. As a non-drinker and somebody who didn't smoke this was going to take some managing, and of course sometimes I fell short. One particular evening, I decided to join some friends at one of the local pubs, deliberating on what would be my drink of choice. Lager made me feel nauseous, spirits would simply get me drunk too quickly and I hadn't yet acquired a taste for wine, but I had occasionally tasted Guinness.

My hope was that one pint of Guinness would last well into the evening, but my friends had other ideas. It appeared to be the custom to try to keep up with the others. I went with stout, which was nicer than I had expected and it seemed that the more I drank, the better it tasted. After about eight pints I was ready, but ready for what? It seemed that at some point during the evening – a point I can't remember – I made my move and proposed to the barmaid. Needless to say, that was the crash and burn of my stout drinking days and I had no further desire to keep up with the Joneses.

The four months I spent in Stoney Stanton are ones I remember with fondness. I met some lovely people and learned a little bit about English village life for the first time.

Into 1989 and things were going well in my world. The Australians were the visiting touring side. It was a campaign perhaps best remembered because England used about 100 different players during the series. At some point, my name was being put forward as a possible Test match player, most probably because the selectors had tried just about everybody else. I couldn't take the thought seriously, or even dare to dream that it could become a reality.

Then, just as my name was appearing in the newspapers, I wasn't fit enough to play. I was suffering with something called Raynaud's Phenomenon, essentially a severe circulation problem. When bowling, the skin on my bowling finger was simply being ripped away by the seam on the ball every time I bowled a delivery. This is a natural part of bowling and normally as the summer progressed the skin on my finger would heal and harden. However, with poor circulation there was simply no healing process so it became progressively worse each time I bowled.

I first noticed it during a county championship game in Bournemouth. It was a warm day but with a bit of a cool breeze coming off the sea. My right hand became frozen solid; it looked purple in colour. I didn't have any feeling in my fingers and I was unable to hold onto the cricket ball. I continued trying to bowl but without much control. Over the next few weeks I tried everything in order to warm my hands but the skin on my bowling finger refused to heal and was getting much worse, I had to stop bowling completely. It was a strange feeling, having the use of your fingers and hands all your life and then, suddenly, it was as if sometimes they weren't even there. I couldn't hold a ball, and only then did I realise how crucial having sensation in the hands and fingers was to bowling. Without that sensation I hadn't got a clue where the ball was going when I let go of it. I would try to hit my lines and lengths but it could easily have been a full toss or a long hop that I delivered. On a good day, it was frustrating and on a bad day I simply wondered how long this would go on for and whether I would ever be able to bowl with confidence again.

The way it was treated was by staying in hospital overnight every six weeks on an intravenous drip, with drugs to improve my circulation. This worked for a while but I did wonder how long I would have to keep going to hospital. And then one day everything was fine again. The extremes of the cold disappeared almost as quickly as they had arrived, although this wasn't until many years later. I still have cold hands and feet, but they no longer freeze over – I am happy to say it's not as severe as it once was.

During that summer of 1989, I took 45 wickets at 21 apiece in the eleven matches I was fit enough to play in and scored 223 championship runs, with a top score of 69, that being my maiden championship 50 against Kent in Folkestone. Then the call came at the end of that season to go with the England A team to Kenya and Zimbabwe. As usual I was surprised. I was still very much caught up with being a county cricketer and I was still, at the time, coming to terms with my Raynaud's condition.

Raynaud's aside, it was time to get down to training. I met up with my new teammates during the winter and we prepared for our adventure. For me, it felt very much like an adventure but I was immensely proud to be included on the tour. I was excited and eager to get out to Africa; more cricket in the winter was just what I wanted, it was better than working as a postman.

But no sooner had I arrived in Kenya than news filtered through that Ricky Ellcock had been injured while with the full England team during their tour to the Caribbean and I was told by our coach, Keith Fletcher, that I needed to fly out to the Caribbean as a replacement. I flew home to London for a couple of days and then caught a flight to the Caribbean. I was so excited. Growing up, my mum never imagined I could ever make a living from playing cricket, let alone represent England. Nobody had thought that I would be good enough to make the grade. I saw my selection as vindication for all the time and effort I had put into my passion of cricket. Despite my mum's desire for me to be a doctor, a dentist or a civil servant of some kind, I knew that she and all my family were going to be very proud of me. I walked around my home turf in Harlesden feeling 10ft tall.

Soon I arrived in Trinidad, a day ahead of the rest of the England team, who were elsewhere in the Caribbean. Initially, I just spent my time soaking up the atmosphere, trying to understand how international players went about their business. Of course, I had always wondered what went on in an international dressing room. How do you prepare for the battle ahead? Well, I soon found out that you train hard, you eat healthily and you get lots of rest. Even though the Caribbean is a beautiful place filled with many beaches, I was not interested in any of that until my job was done. The socialising would have to wait.

Soon after, the rest of the squad joined up and preparations for our first match began. My schoolmate Phil DeFreitas sustained a twisted knee during practice, which resulted in a like-for-like replacement, one all-rounder for another. I found myself walking out onto the pitch with my teammates on my 22nd birthday – Valentine's Day 1990. I strolled out onto the field at the Queen's Park Oval to make my debut for England. This was even more special because it was in the Caribbean, not far from where I had been born and raised in Guyana, where much of my extended family still lived.

The day I first pulled on an England shirt is still hard to describe. I was tingling with excitement, and even now as I write this I can remember the occasion vividly – the noise, the colours, the smells all added to the sensation. And we were playing the legendary West Indies team, led by the great Viv Richards, with opening batsmen Gordon Greenidge and Desmond Haynes. These guys had been greats for as long as I could remember. They were playing in front of what seemed like 30–40,000 people. The West Indies had been at the top of world cricket for a decade or more, beating everyone. Now I was lining up against them.

But the England captain, Graham Gooch, was a titan. He was a battler, a warrior. As a young boy, I had listened to him on the radio giving those great West Indian bowlers more than a good run for their money. The others – Allan Lamb, Robin Smith, Angus Fraser and Jack Russell – I had played against at county level. Those I did not know personally, but I still knew of them.

It was a warm and sunny day and the Queen's Park Oval was like a cauldron. The crowd was loud and excitable, the colours in the stadium seemed to be extra bright, the music pumping, steel pans, the smell of roti in the air and of course the dancing – I loved it, it was my sort of place. It might have been distracting for some, but for me it just created more atmosphere, more energy. And in the midst of it, what else would you want to be doing apart from playing cricket?

This is how I grew up in the Caribbean, playing my cricket. I had dreamt of this moment, taking the field for England, and here I was – not amongst the spectators, but amongst the players. I was one of the people the crowd had come to watch. Even as a young boy, I had imagined what this must be like and childhood memories came flooding back to me. I remembered standing under a tree with my friends watching a shooting star. You had to make a wish and not tell anyone, otherwise it would not come true. As a 7-year-old I had wished for two things: one was to go to England, the other was to play cricket. I did not specify playing cricket for England, but plainly if you want to go there and you want to play cricket the rest must follow, and here I was ticking off the very top item on my wish list. To be honest, if I didn't score a run or take a wicket, it didn't matter. Just to be there, turning out for England, would have been enough.

We won the toss and Goochy decided the home team should bat first. Gladstone Small and Angus Fraser opened the bowling and I was put in the outfield where the ball was likely to go, mainly because I was a decent runner and a good fielder. In those days I was a bit of whippet and I was one of the half a dozen who were able-bodied. I was in my element and this was a day, more than any other, to show what I could do on the cricket field.

There was a huge roar from an expectant crowd when Greenidge and Haynes came out to bat. Their idea was a simple one: they were going to smash us to all parts of the ground. That's what they were there for and the steel pans ramped up the excitement. I remember Haynes going after Fraser, the steel drums pumping up the noise as the bowler ran in. Then there was an explosion when the batsman hit the ball for 4, which subsided to a bubbling chatter as the bowler walked back to his mark before the build-up began again. For me, all that noise was 101 per cent stimulation.

Greenidge and Haynes made a watchful start in the end, scoring 26 runs off the first 10 overs. When Fraser and Small took a break, I came on with David Capel. To be honest, I was a little bit overawed. There was a moment just before I bowled my first bowl, I turned and here I was about to bowl at none other than my childhood hero, Gordon Greenidge – the man I had pretended to be when playing as a child. It was mad. It had gone beyond a dream now. It had never occurred to me that one day I would be bowling to Greenidge and his legendary opening partner, Desmond Haynes. But here I was on an island not half an hour's plane journey away from where I was born doing that very thing. It seemed like serendipity.

It was an emotional moment. Even in my wildest dreams, I could never have imagined that I would be bowling to these giants, here on the same pitch as my childhood heroes. It was simply incredible, surely this was heaven. How could it get better than this? But I was going to have to get a grip; I couldn't show the batsmen such emotions. As a novice, I knew the West Indian top order would see me as a weak link and they'd be after me. But with the second ball of my first over, Greenidge played forward to one, it nipped back and hit him on middle. I humbly suggested that he was out, out, out – leg before wicket. A big shout went up. I turned and looked at the umpire but he shook his head. I remember walking back to my mark, I was distraught. But then it occurred to me – hang on, I know the umpire didn't give it but you just got Gordon Greenidge out!

Even so, Haynes seemed determined to take me on. He kept running down the wicket, trying to hit the new boy out of the ground. The question was, what should I do next? Should I bowl the next ball in the same place, or should I try something different?

One of the things I had learned about batsmen is that, if they are trying something out of the ordinary, you must be having some effect on them. I figured that the reason Haynes was running down the wicket was because I was making things difficult for him. That convinced me to keep bowling in the same place. It paid off. In my fourth over, Haynes jabbed at one just outside the off stump and edged it to the keeper. He was out, caught behind, and I had my first international wicket. Haynes – no, Desmond Haynes – caught Russell, bowled Lewis for 25.

I bowled 7 overs, with one of them being a maiden, for figures of 1 for 30. But there was still a lot of hero-worshipping going on when Viv Richards sauntered to the crease, as only he could – well, what do you say to Viv Richards? Nothing if you're a bowler and have got any sense – did he even know who I was? Richards was soon smashing Eddie Hemmings into the stands for 6.

My contribution to the game was not over yet. I was on the long-on boundary when Ezra Moseley hit one my way. As I looked up at the ball, I could feel the crowd's eyes on me, so I steadied myself and made sure I caught it. It was Ezra's debut too and he was out for 2 runs. After 50 overs, West Indies were 208 for 8.

Soon after the interval, rain swept in from the hills behind the ground. It went on for ninety minutes and the game was abandoned with England on 26 for 1. We had been batting for only 13 overs, 2 short of the mandatory 15, before a result could be declared. The score didn't bother me, nor did it bother me that I didn't get to bat. I only remember the sunshine, the excitement, the emotion and the pride.

For me, it was the most complete day of my life. Everything seemed to have fallen into place that day: playing cricket in the road outside my gran's house in Georgetown; my uncle spending $5 on a ball; moving to England at the age of 10, where I could continue developing my game while my friends in Guyana had to find work; the school sports masters who encouraged me; becoming a British subject; and Ken, who saw my potential. If any one of those things had not happened, I may not have been there on the field playing for England on that glorious day in Trinidad.

After the match, back in the hotel, I was bouncing off the walls. Even today, when I think back, I struggle to contain the emotions and put them into words. I had achieved what I had set out to do – playing for England against the West Indies – and I had dismissed Haynes! As it was to turn out, this wouldn't be enough, but at that very moment I was completely made up.

My family was proud too. They, like many from the Caribbean, did not often show their pride outwardly but I knew they were there for me. I could only imagine what my extended family would have made of it all back in Guyana. My gran, uncles and aunts all thought 'little Chrissy' was a star from the day I was born. I owed my relatives in Georgetown so much. They had got me started and I knew that they would have been extremely proud of what I had achieved so far. I would have loved to play for England in Guyana, but I was just very happy to be here. This was as good as it got, but it would change later. I came onto the tour with no real expectations hanging over me but, of course, the more I did on the field, the larger those expectations became.

In another tour match, I was 12th man and, whilst carrying some drinks around the boundary for the bowlers, I got some stick from the locals. They kept shouting, 'Hey, Chris man, they brought you all the way back to the Caribbean as a waiter.' It made me smile. Then, later in the day I was on the field as a substitute and was at fine leg right in front of the same group of guys; the chatter continued. At the end of the day's play, I was walking off the field and I saw the group jump over the fence, heading in my direction; I quickened up my pace, thinking I didn't really want any more of this. Then one of them shouted out, 'Chris, Chris, don't run away man! We want to talk to you.' So, I slowed down my walk so they could catch up.

'Chris, we want you to know something,' one of them said. 'We are very proud of you playing for England, do the very best you can.' He went on to say, 'we will be back here tomorrow doing the same thing, but don't take it too seriously man – it's just cricket.' That put everything into the right order for me. The people of the Caribbean were proud of me, even though I was playing for my adopted country and not theirs. As a replacement, I didn't play much on the rest of the tour. A second One Day International in Trinidad was again ruined by the weather and then I was replaced by Phil DeFreitas for the next two games after he returned from injury. With us 2–0 down and only one game of a five-match series remaining, I was picked again for a game in Barbados, but bowled only 5 expensive overs. I was not chosen for any of the following Test matches, but just being there, in that international atmosphere in the Caribbean around those players, was an unforgettable experience.

Off the field, I was just as happy with my life. I had lots of music with me and in the evenings, I would have a dance in my hotel room listening to my favourite artists. I think I was probably also caught busting a couple of moves on the cricket field from time to time.

The routine was to be at the ground early, and so I would be there for ten or eleven hours during the day, around the cricket environment. I don't know why this has surprised so many people over the years but, as much as I loved the game, there were things I also enjoyed outside of it. In most other jobs, work isn't all consuming, and for me, as a professional sportsman, I liked to separate what was work and what wasn't. Sometimes that meant getting away from cricket, both physically and mentally.

Given my background, how I spent my social time was very different to the way most of my teammates did. I didn't drink and so didn't enjoy pubs; I had spent too much time in club cricket, after matches waiting in bars for someone to take me home – but I did like dancing. I also had lots of friends outside of cricket: people I had grown up with, and wanted to spend time with them when I could. So, when the day's play was over, I often slipped away to be by myself or with friends. Having already spent nearly twelve hours at the cricket ground, I was normally ready to get away. I wanted to do something else.

The 1980s came to an end and the '90s could not have started any better for me. I found on my return that there had been changes at Leicestershire. Bob Simpson had come in as coach and, although I didn't realise it at the time, he too was to have an influence on my cricket. Bob was very keen on fielding practice and he brought in lots of different fielding drills. He helped me to improve, especially my slip catching.

The 1990 season began with a championship match in Cardiff against Glamorgan, who had Viv Richards as their overseas player. Alan Mullally had Viv in a bit of trouble. He was beating the outside edge and the great man looked surprisingly uncomfortable. I remember running over to Al and saying to him, 'You can get him here, you really can'.

In typical fashion, Mullally retorted, 'Man, I don't know how I can bowl to this guy, I've got a picture of him on my wall!'

I understood what he was saying – this was Viv Richards after all – but I did laugh at Al's approach. I got Viv out, bowled him, and took 6 for 55, along with 4 for 64 in the second innings, and we won the game easily. Viv struck a hundred in the second innings, before I dismissed him again, but when we chatted after the game we talked only about my batting. I'd made 39, which Viv said showed promise. He then gave me a gem. He told me that once the bowler had delivered the ball and it's dead, don't look at him: pay no attention to him.

'Clear your head,' he told me, 'take a stroll, head to the beach in your mind.'

This meant that the actual time you have to concentrate while batting is minute in comparison. If you spend too much time watching the bowler, what will happen is that you will try to figure out what he will bowl to you next. Only look at him as he starts to run in at you again – the rest is a waste of mental energy.

In the very next game we were at Chelmsford and I struck my maiden first-class hundred. My previous highest score had been 69 and I ended the first day of the match on 57, on a pitch that was flat and hard. The weather was very hot for that time of year and runs were being scored right across the country. In the same round of fixtures, Surrey amassed more than 700 in their first innings and yet still conceded a lead of 150-plus, thanks to a triple hundred from Neil Fairbrother.

Mine was not a faultless innings by any means. I was dropped a couple of times, but then I made it to three figures. I had done it, and it was a large hundred, too. I ended unbeaten on 189 – my old mate, Mullally, unable to stay with me to see me to a double ton.

I followed that up with an undefeated 93, as we defeated Essex in a Sunday League match. So, in the space of a week, straight after that conversation with Viv Richards, I had scored almost 300 runs without getting out. All the things I had learned in practice were now bearing fruit.

Back in the county game, I had noticed that the batsmen were now treating my bowling with a lot more respect. In fact, all aspects of my game were on the rise. I had very much enjoyed myself around the England team but I wasn't expecting to be included in any squads for the Summer's series with New Zealand. I was fully aware that I had to perform, and all my focus was on doing that for Leicestershire. But, as it turned out, I was included in the England team for the third Test at Edgbaston. Phil DeFreitas was ill and so I was told that I was going to make my Test debut.

It was, of course, a very big moment. For those who want to put a timeframe on this, I remember that the traditional pre-match dinner was abandoned in favour of a buffet so the players could watch the football World Cup semi-final between England and West Germany in Italy. My Test debut came on 5 July 1990. I was 22.

I batted at number 8; coming in after Graham Gooch had scored a big hundred. I was pleased that I stuck it out in the middle for more than an hour and a half, batting with Jack Russell and Gladstone Small in making 32. My maiden Test match wicket was that of the great Martin Crowe who I trapped

LBW, although he didn't like umpire Barry Meyer's decision very much. Crowe initially didn't look at Meyer's raised finger and he had to be given out a second time. I ended with figures of 1 for 51 from 19 overs in an innings dominated by Eddie Hemmings, whose 6 wickets put us in control of the match. In the second innings, I became one of Sir Richard Hadlee's last ever victims in what was his final Test appearance and claimed 3 for 76, as we won the match by 114 runs. It had been a wonderful experience, making my Test debut, and at the end of the game to have been part of a winning England team.

In truth, my debut in Trinidad had felt more important. I know this was Test cricket, and it is the ultimate challenge for any professional cricketer – it is the form of cricket where you have to be mentally and physically tough and fit – but for me playing international cricket for England was my high. Of course, I was very proud of making my Test debut, but it was the day in Trinidad the previous winter which really sticks in my memory. This was simply a beautiful time and I was enjoying myself a great deal. I played cricket and I played it well. Everything I could think of was wrapped up in playing the sport I had dreamt of playing. On the pitch, I was having a lot of fun and once the work was done I could go out and enjoy myself. Music, dancing and the opposite sex were my passions away from cricket.

The money I was now making was by no means astronomical, but it was a decent amount for a young man and I enjoyed spending it and sharing it, through gifts, with family and friends I grew up with. I bought lots of music, nice clothes, cars and apartments, and had no problem spending what I was earning. I was by no means rich – no cricketer was then – but I was comfortable. We enjoyed life together, buying nice things to enhance the experience. This was just the life I wanted at the age of 22. In fact, looking back, the only regret I have is that I didn't enjoy myself more. I did my best, though, to live my dreams, and this was certainly the golden time of my life.

Was I the consummate professional? No, I could have stayed in a bit more, thinking about or watching more cricket, but I was having a ball. I worked hard, trained a lot – although it never felt like work because I enjoyed it so much – and when that was done it was time for fun, heading off to a club or to a concert. It meant that I was sometimes tired when performing, of course, but this rarely seemed to affect what I did on the field. There were the occasional mishaps, but nothing was terminal.

I had gone from playing cricket for Wembley, only a couple of years before, to this life. I started to have to come up with new aspirations on a daily basis, as so many were ticked off in a short space of time. I had not spent five years in the second team at Leicestershire, working my way up the ladder. For me, I just got out and played my cricket and the rest took care of itself.

My friends were proud of what I was achieving. We had grown up together and had our dreams together. Some, like Ian Ervine, my vice-captain at Willesden High, tasted his: having a year with Gloucestershire. People now asked me for my autograph, which I found strange but flattering and still do. I didn't think that I was any different to anybody else, so why would anyone want me to sign something? I never thought of it as a chore, but it was an odd and new experience for me.

Women were part of this new chapter. I was young and I was single and so what better time? A serious relationship did not seem to work with the schedule of a professional cricketer. I could not offer stability, and when there was an emotional commitment required, I was usually emotionally committed to my cricket, which came first. I was on the road or abroad for half of the winter, restricting my availability for any kind of serious relationship. I did try though. I was staying in five-star hotels with extensive travel and I lapped it up – but nothing is ever perfect. Away from my friends, the lack of me jumping on groupies or picking up women in nightclubs while out with my teammates seemed to convince them that I was gay. In the dressing room, it was the unspoken thought hanging in the air. It was never brought up openly, but there are no real secrets in any dressing room. On one occasion, a teammate approached a friend of mine at the ground and asked him if I was gay. He knew that my friend would tell me, so I suppose that is as close as I ever got to an actual accusation. The truth of it was that, in the evenings after a match, I hung out with my friends outside of cricket, and did little socialising with my teammates. That may have fuelled the rumours. I still have to deal with that question today from cricketers: who have you been talking to?

I was a little hurt by the gay rumours, especially as it was a time when few sportsmen had come out and rumours of that nature had the potential to harm a career. What did what I got up to in the evenings, away from the ground, have to do with anybody? I chose not to focus on the matter, as it had no bearing on my ability to play cricket.

You might remember that one of the main things I learned from my mother early on was not to follow the actions of others or concern myself with what they were up to. It was hard sticking to this the way things were. I was learning on the job and discovering that in a dressing room you are not always going to get on with people. There is a perception that these rooms are all filled with kindred spirits, everybody playing cricket together and getting on at every moment, sharing this great adventure. That's great – it's romantic – it's also very rarely true. You may be a successful dressing room, but half the people in it have a different way of doing things. The only important thing, of course, is that all eleven have the same goals: to win matches. Having not long left the Caribbean, the idea that I would not always fit in with everybody was always the most likely outcome.

There didn't seem to be the same issues in the England dressing room, where I was the new boy sitting alongside the likes of Allan Lamb, Robin Smith and Graham Gooch. All these guys had achieved plenty and were confident men, so they had no need to pay as much attention to what I was doing. They had their own things to get on with, their own plans and achievements to fulfil.

Gooch's methods were not my methods, but he worked so hard at his game and all that work paid off. Just look at his stats, they are fantastic. He was a good leader – he lead from the front. I would put him and Peter Willey very much into the same category. He scored big hundreds and lots of them; you can only admire him for that. He never took a step back; he never shirked any of his responsibilities. He just got on with things in an unflustered manner – a proper soldier. My friendship with Robin Smith was one of the most meaningful of those with any of my professional teammates. I am very fond of him and his family. They are very nice people. Robin hit a cricket ball as hard as anyone, especially if you were stupid enough to bowl short and outside the off stump at him. If you did that, the ball would disappear in a flash. His strength and his sense of adventure were among the many things I admired about him. He would never back down, whatever the challenge he faced. I would like to take this point in the book to convey my sincere thanks to Robin and his wife Kathy for the support and friendship they have shown me throughout my professional career, particularly during my prison sentence. Kathy never forgot a birthday.

The remainder of the 1992 international summer saw me play two more Tests at Lord's and Old Trafford, both against India. I remember spending a lot of my time in the dressing room as Graham Gooch scored run after run after run. The highlight for me were the wicket of the young Sachin Tendulkar, who scored his first Test hundred in the second innings in Manchester to save the game for India.

Meanwhile, back with Leicestershire, I completed the season with 700 first-class runs and more than 50 first-class wickets. This was enough to see me included in the squad for the tour of Australia – a milestone for me. I had been included in the squad in the Caribbean the previous year, but only as a replacement for Ricky Elcock, while my Test debut had come due to an illness of Phil DeFreitas. So, this was the first time that I had been selected for what I had personally achieved.

I remember being with England in Australia, and we hadn't started the first Test match. We were just playing one of the local games and we had finished the day. We'd had a bowl and tomorrow we would be a batting day, and in those days that was a cue for a night out. So, I got back to the hotel, had a Chinese takeaway and by eight o'clock I was in my bed, fast asleep.

The alarm was set for eleven o'clock. I got up at eleven and woke up my partner in crime (sorry, Devon!). We were going to have a night out, listen to a bit of music and experience a bit of Australia; we'd only just got there. As we walked out of the front of the hotel, there was a cab coming in, so we decided we'd take it. We got to the door of the car to open it and let the people out, so we could jump in, only to discover that it was the captain, Graham Gooch, and manager, Mickey Stewart. So, there we were, about to pretend that we were tired and had just arrived back and were heading in to the hotel. They both looked at us, laughed, and said, 'Get on your way!' We jumped in the taxi and had a couple of hours out, enjoyed a bit of music and got away from the pressures of the game. We got to be ourselves for a while, and were able to appreciate where we were. We returned to the hotel to finish our sleep and then I was up to play the following morning – just doing my thing, I felt young and strong enough at this time.

By the opening Test match of the series in Brisbane I was ready to go. I was thrilled that it was in Australia, a country I had really enjoyed visiting for the Youth World Cup. I loved the place and its people, their matter-of-fact attitude and their up-and-at-'em approach to life. I would visit Australia many times over the years, just to enjoy the country and its outdoor lifestyle.

The first Test, however, was a disappointment and we lost heavily. Not entirely surprising, as Australia were the best team in the world at that time. We were hoping to improve in the second Test in Melbourne, but there was a question mark over my fitness: I was experiencing a dull pain in my back. I was not in agony, just discomfort. It seemed to be a minor problem for the most part. But, experience had already taught me that if I rested for a few days an injury would generally start to show some form of improvement. This, however, was to be quite different. Even after resting for three or four days there was no change. As soon as I bowled in the nets, the pain was there – from ball one there was no change. When I was resting it felt fine, but the moment I delivered a ball I would feel that dull pain in my back – no improvement even with treatment.

I was sent for an MRI in Melbourne, where they found a crack in my lower back. Being diagnosed with a stress fracture was a frightening moment. The player I replaced in the West Indies, Ricky Ellcock, had suffered the same injury and it marked the end of his cricket career. It was difficult not to make a comparison and I wondered whether my career was at an end before it had even started. There was a certain amount of panic. Within a few days, I was on a plane back home, the tour quickly over for me. At least I knew that my problem had been diagnosed early and the gap between the bones was not too severe, which meant that there was no need for surgery, just prolonged rest. This would heal on its own with two or three months of inactivity, lying on my back at home.

Thankfully, that worked. Three months later, the follow-up scan showed that the back had healed. It was a good result and a relief, as stress fractures for bowlers can be terminal to their careers. I was beginning to realise that any sportsman's career does not just rise and that there will be problems along the way, whether it be through injury, a lack of form, the desertion of Lady Luck or indeed, sometimes in my case, stupidity!

I was fortunate, and was declared fit enough to play in the first championship game of the season. It went very well as, in a rain-affected match, I took 5 for 35 from 22 overs. However, I was in pain. The dull ache in my back returned and I was back at the doctors for another scan. This affected my cricket in the first half of that summer. Thankfully, that scan was all clear, and after missing one match against Nottinghamshire I returned for the next game in Northampton, but I was unable to play in successive matches. After bowling it just felt like the injury was there again.

Sometimes, when an injury physically gets better, the pain can still be there. Muscles are tight and weak, having not been used for a while, and so with overexertion they can still cause some pain. I guess that was what I was experiencing after a long layoff in the winter.

Back on the cricket field, I just had to play through it, and eventually my back got stronger while playing. Sometimes playing through the pain can be difficult to do – you don't always know if you are going to do more damage. However, this was going to be a patchy season, with some matches played and other matches missed altogether.

The low point of the summer was being selected for the first Test of the season against the West Indies only to be taken ill on the eve of the game. But the high point was definitely returning for the last two Tests at Edgbaston and the Oval. In the first of these, I took my best bowling figures in international cricket of 6 for 111, as well as making my highest Test score at the time of 65, batting at number 10 in a game we still lost. The World Cup was just around the corner and yet more dreams were about to become a reality.

6

THE 1992 WORLD CUP
AND A NEW CAREER

By the time we headed out to New Zealand at the start of 1992, I was often being hailed in the media as the 'new Ian Botham'. This didn't mean much to me, because – here was the thing – I was not Ian Botham. But what it led to was an expectation from the outside that I should be performing like the great all-rounder. I took this as a compliment, of course, but other than that, I never really thought about it.

You get it in all sports, this guy being the new David Beckham or Tiger Woods, and each will deal with that in their own way. I just ignored it for the most part, although I must admit that I did style some of my game on Botham when I was younger – every all-rounder did, I'm sure, whether it was the way they ran into bowl, the way they jumped up before letting go of the ball, or the way they set themselves up in the crease when batting.

I admired Botham more as a bowler. He had such great skill – swinging the ball both ways. Who wouldn't want control like that? As a young boy growing up, he influenced me because he was the best in the world at what he did. He was one of the giants I used to hear about on the radio, and it was an odd experience to find myself in the same dressing room as him.

The first Test on this important tour was at Christchurch where I made 70, batting at number 8. England won by an innings, with Phil Tufnell getting 11 wickets in the match after Alec Stewart had struck a hundred on the opening day. I got through 52 overs in the match.

In the second Test match, it was with the ball that I came good, taking 5 for 31 in the first innings in Auckland. Once again, we won handsomely.

I missed out on the third and final Test, being rested and replaced by David 'Syd' Lawrence at the Basin Reserve in Wellington. That was a match mostly remembered for Big Syd's horrific knee injury. I was back in the hotel, watching the cricket on the TV in my room. I saw Syd running into bowl, all 18 stone of him, a big and very strong man, who was very proud of his strength. He was certainly not the kind of man who would squeal to show that he was suffering from any pain. The ground was only about a mile away from where I was, and although I had the TV on, I could swear that the scream of agony I heard, came from outside the window, right from the Basin Reserve itself.

Syd had banged his leg down in his bowling stride and essentially the muscles inside his leg had ripped his kneecap apart. Half was down near his ankle and the other half was up near his thigh. I can't even imagine such an injury, and just how much pain he would be in. I quickly put my clothes on and headed down to the ground, and when I got there Syd was being put into an ambulance. I jumped in and sat with him, knowing that surely this was the end of his career, one which appeared to have been finished off doing exactly what I had done thousands of times – just running in to bowl. How could doing that have this sort of effect? It gave plenty of room for thought.

Quickly, all who witnessed that horrific event had to get over it and move on. You just have to.

We took the series 2–0, which was a great effort as the Black Caps had a strong side: especially at home, which was warming up for the World Cup due to be held in both their own country and in Australia.

We prepared for that by winning the One Day Series convincingly too. The third and final match was back in Christchurch where the pitch was totally different to the one we had played the Test match on. I couldn't get my run-up right at all, whatever I tried; yet somehow the ball was coming out of my hand with real venom. Alec Stewart was standing well back behind the stumps. I hit John Wright on the head and caused problems for all the other batsmen. It was the first time I had seen a speed gun at a ground and it said I was touching 90mph. I thought that I couldn't possibly be bowling at that pace, as I couldn't even get my run-up or rhythm right. I kept trying to correct things to see how quickly I could deliver the ball but that never happened as now I was trying too hard.

Apart from that, I was ready, and after a good time in New Zealand the whole team was prepared for the World Cup, which began for us across the water in Perth against India, just a week later. We had a good team and had prepared well, with the likes of Gooch, Botham, Smith, Lamb, Fairbrother, Reeve, Hick,

DeFreitas, Pringle and Stewart all looking hungry. Everybody could bat and it seemed that everybody could bowl. We had a lot of options on the field.

We started the tournament on a winning note by beating India in Perth – Robin Smith with 91 helping us to a final score of 236 for 9 from our 50 overs, which was 9 runs too many for the Indians. My own contribution was 10 runs with the bat and 0 for 36 with the ball. Next up, we travelled to Melbourne, a city I had already visited many times, but this time it was for a World Cup game and there seemed to be a special buzz around the place. There, we took on the West Indies and won with more than 10 overs to spare, dismissing them for just 157, those runs being knocked off for the loss of 4 wickets, with half-centuries for Gooch and Hick. My contribution was figures of 3 for 30, for which I was named Man of the Match.

I was in Australia, playing for England in a World Cup, winning matches and winning Man of the Match awards. I was in a great place and looking forward to the rest of the competition.

Next up, to Adelaide to meet Pakistan. They were led by the caged tiger himself, Imran Khan, a man who I had greatly admired throughout his career. His pace, his flair, his swing, his swagger were all great qualities. Pakistan were formidable opposition, although they had not been performing at their best in this tournament, even with the likes of Imran, Wasim Akram, Waqar Younis, Javed Miandad and a young Inzamam-ul-Haq.

We won the toss and put them in. From the gully, I watched a procession of wickets. They batted for 40 overs but could only muster a total of 74, Pringle with 3 for 8 from 8 overs and Botham 2 for 12 from 10. The pitch certainly aided these skilled bowlers, but it was more like a 150-run wicket. Everything, however, went our way. Even though it was a small total to chase, we knew it wasn't going to be easy with Wasim and Aaqib Javed running in with the new white ball, but we were obviously very confident of knocking off the 75 runs we required to make it three wins from three.

We got to 24 for 1 after 8 overs, but it was suddenly not looking good. The Adelaide Oval was enveloped in dark clouds and the heavens looked as if they were just about to open. In a short time, it became clear that we were not going to play again after the rain started.

Unlucky, I guess, but we had them. Who would be able to tell at that stage of the competition that the one point gained by our opposition would make all the difference to them and the tournament.

Four days later, we were in Sydney for the biggest game yet, against co-hosts Australia. This was the one. We were all pumped. It was a good time to play them. We were in form and, from where I sat, everybody was confident in the ability of his teammates to put in a match-changing contribution. But, before I could get into it, my intercostal was playing up. I had tried to bowl quickly in the game against the West Indies and I had strained it a bit – in fact, I had strained it a lot. I was able to roll the ball out of my hand, but not deliver it with any real pace. I hadn't bowled in the match with Pakistan – I hadn't needed to – so on the morning of the Australia game, I had to prove my fitness. It wasn't so much proving my fitness as saying I was fit and capable of bowling with some pace. With the aid of an injection in my side, surely, I could get through 10 overs.

I walked out onto the old ground in Sydney. I don't know why, but this ground has to be my favourite in the whole world. The atmosphere, the green roofs, or maybe it was because I had watched *Bodyline* too much as a kid. Whatever it was, the atmosphere in the ground always made me tingle, even more so on this day. I started to jog around the ground with my teammates. A section of England supporters were in there early. There were only about 100 of them, but as we ran around and got close to them, they started to make a tremendous noise. They were so passionate and desperate for us to beat Australia. I hadn't experienced anything like this before – not the noise, but the energy that their passion gave me. By the end of the lap, I knew I had to play and be part of what was going to be a fantastic day. It was the first time that I could say, tangibly, that I got energy from the crowd. In one moment, I wasn't sure if I could play, but in the next, I knew I had to.

Australia won the toss and batted, but were dismissed for 171 with Botham leading the way again, with 4 for 31. He also struck a 50 as we made 173 for 2, reaching the winning line with 55 balls to spare. What a feeling – thrashing Australia in Sydney in a World Cup game! My effort saw me produce economical figures of 0–28 from my 10 overs, I didn't let them get away. But, my side was still painful. Even with a cortisone injection, it still didn't feel as if I could bowl through my action with any strength or any real purpose. My side felt fragile, but thanks to the injection it was not hurting as much.

However, my injury was a minor thought at this moment as I stood on the balcony in Sydney, taking in the atmosphere.

Everybody was buzzing – the players, the spectators – and even by midnight, when it was still very warm, we hadn't left the ground.

The mood in our camp was good as we headed to Ballarat for our next contest against Sri Lanka. We won the toss and batted first and made 280 for 6 with 50s for Fairbrother and Stewart and most of the other batsmen contributing, with 40s from Botham and Hick and a little cameo from myself of 20 off 6 balls. Sri Lanka replied with 174 and we had won yet again. There was another Man of the Match award for myself as I took 4 for 30, removing the top four batsmen. We were a good team, playing good cricket. When it was this way, somebody always came to the party.

It seemed like everything was going well, but it wasn't really. This day had been one of those days when batsmen hit the ball to fielders and those fielders took good catches off bad balls. I was bowling line and length, but if a batsman was to run at me I didn't have a higher gear to move into. Thank God this was not Twenty20! This was getting rather annoying. There is nothing more frustrating than being on a cricket field and wanting to show what you can do but not being able to, through injury or some restriction in your body. I was so frustrated with my body.

The day worked out, but there would be harder challenges ahead when it wouldn't be so easy. Up stepped South Africa in the next game. These guys had been starved of international cricket for a very long time because of the boycott of South

African sport due to apartheid. It was the first meeting between England and the South Africans since 1965. They were hungry and ready to prove a point. There would certainly be no quarter given in this game.

I was not fit enough to bowl, and there were other guys in the squad waiting for their chance to play. Luckily, I was then thrown a lifeline. The conversation was that I could play as a batsman only, allowing me to run around in the field to save as many runs as I could, maybe 20 or so, and then being able to contribute with the bat in the lower order. So, it was decided that even though I couldn't bowl, I was worth my place in the starting XI. What a result!

We won the toss and stuck them in. South Africa made a good start, with Kepler Wessels and Andrew Hudson sharing an opening stand of 151, but they ended up only getting 236 for 4 from their 50 overs. Pringle, the most economical of the bowlers, again with 0 for 34 from 9 overs. I chased everything that came anywhere near me on the cover boundary, where I had spent the afternoon covering yards. Without having to bowl, I could use up all my energy in the field.

In reply, we started off at a good rate – 62 for 0 from 12 overs – and then the rain came. This was the first time I had been introduced in a meaningful way to Duckworth/Lewis. I didn't understand it; in total, 11 runs were taken off the target but crucially 9 overs were lost. We were left to get 160 more runs from 29 overs, the new run rate rapidly increased – plus a pitch which had been spruced up by the rain which was not going to help us. A score of 62 for 0 quickly became 64 for 3, with Botham, Smith and Hick all gone; but there was plenty of batting still to come. Fairbrother and Stewart did an excellent job of repairing the damage, and also kept the run rate up. They put on 68 in 13 overs to keep us in the game.

Stewart was then run out for 77 – a fantastic knock, and he was soon followed back to the pavilion by Dermot Reeve for 10, the score now 166 for 5, with 60 needed. It was going to be tight. I had had all day to wait and prepare for my part, and now here it was. If there were anybody I would like to have batted with in this kind of situation it would have been Neil 'Harvey' Fairbrother. I had watched him bat many times, both in county cricket and for England. There was a knowledge around the game that when Harvey's eyes went, then the bowlers needed to watch out. When he was in the zone, those eyes had a glazed appearance and you knew that fireworks were about to happen.

I got to the crease and I saw that intensity in his eyes. He was up for it. I knew that if I could stay around a while, taking a couple of overs just to get my own eye in, we could do this. A couple of inside edges for 4 and then finally one off the middle over cover. I was into my stride, and we were running hard and scoring runs at every opportunity. In what seemed like no time at all, we had added 50 runs in 6 overs and the game was within site.

Now we just had to cross the line. Adrenalin was pumping. I wandered halfway down the wicket from the non-striker's end, pushing my luck just a bit too far. It was Jonty Rhodes at backward point, and I was run out by yards, disappointed not to be there at the end, but I enjoyed that knock. With 33 runs coming off my bat from 22 balls and 10 still needed, there were 2 overs to go, with Pringle, DeFreitas, Illingworth and Gladstone Small still to come. We won with one ball to spare: Fairbrother 75 not out. The odds had been stacked against us, but we had done it! This was what cricket was all about. It was yet another great night. I had played my part in an unforgettable victory.

As I said, the management had told me that my job was to save runs in the field and score handily with the bat. I did both. But a couple of days later, I started to hear that there were doubts from others within the team as to whether I actually had a side strain at all. Apparently, I moved too well in the field for that to be the case – according to some of the boys. I was called into a meeting with Graham Gooch who told me that this was the opinion being expressed.

My thoughts right at that moment when I heard that were, 'Just fuck off.' I didn't say anything, just thought, 'What is the fucking matter with you lot?' If I didn't want to play, I wouldn't have played – but why wouldn't I have wanted to? I loved playing. I was asked to do a job and I did it as best as I could, and now, because I had done it well, I was getting a load of shit. I was fuming, but remained calm, instead listening to the drivel that was being said to me. 'You moved too well to be injured,' was one comment. What was I supposed to do, hold my side while I ran? It was a load of crap.

This incident soured what had been a great game. I had done everything that was asked of me and now I had to deal with this bullshit. I began to feel that this was becoming a bit of a pattern. In certain situations, I felt that I couldn't win. It had been the same before my stress fracture in Australia had been confirmed.

There again, people thought that I couldn't be injured because I moved too well. Now, the bigwigs were at it again. Everybody else could be injured, but if I was, then I must be faking. This appeared to come from general observations of my movement.

I was getting a lot of stick that a lot of other players didn't seem to get and a lot of this, according to people, was my unwillingness to play, my laziness and a low pain threshold. I was constantly being told that I was a natural athlete and moved well. What I was beginning to learn was that, even when injured, I seemed to move too well. Yet I did not come out of my mother as an athlete. The way I moved was due in part to the lifestyle I had growing up. I remember that I never played inside the house – I wasn't allowed to – so play was always outside until it got too dark. I was constantly climbing trees, running, throwing stones and doing cartwheels. This was how I played, but it was also good training for what was to come later in my life. In Guyana, this was normal for all the children. We would all run around, jumping here and jumping there. We rode our bikes, played cricket – all active enjoyment with no board games or anything like that. All our fun was physical. When I was starting my career and some people would make comments on my athleticism, I would think to myself, 'What on earth are they talking about?' I wasn't even the most agile out of my group of friends.

For me, it was a form of discrimination, because I was athletic and moved well; even when injured, I simply couldn't have an injury.

In the end, I just got on with it because that was my job. Despite this, I was enjoying the tournament. I was not asked to play because of my side injury in the low-scoring surprise loss to Zimbabwe, but I was back for the semi-final against South Africa in Sydney.

We posted a reasonable score thanks to 83 from Graeme Hick and I batted towards the end to get us up to 252 for 6 from our 45 overs, adding 34 in quick time with Dermot Reeve. We remained ahead of the game with the ball, too, until South Africa began to fight back through Jonty Rhodes, Brian McMillan and David Richardson. It was even-stevens when the rain arrived, with South Africa on 231 for 6, needing 22 more off 13 balls. We needed a couple of wickets, I was bowling at the time, but here comes the rain. A shower took us off the field for all of twelve minutes. What followed next was not too dissimilar to our previous meeting in the group stages – with the side batting second now up against it.

Essentially, the overs that were taken off by the rain-affected system back then were maiden overs or ones with the fewest runs. So, the South Africans lost two overs, while the target was hardly reduced. We famously came back out for one ball, by which time the target had been reduced to 21 runs. We were initially confused when we returned to the field, thinking that there was 1 over and 1 ball for South Africa to get the runs they required. But while we were on the pitch it was made clear to us that, in fact, there was only one delivery of the match to go. I ran in, bowled that ball at a slow medium pace, McMillan taking a single to mid-wicket – and there we were, in the World Cup final.

I was jubilant. I didn't care about how the game ended. That was South Africa's problem not ours, and, as I have said, we had won against the odds when the rain fell in our group game. A lot of people were sad and up in arms about it, but I did not give a monkey's. I didn't get what the South Africans were moaning about. They knew the rules; their over rate had been so slow during our innings that we lost 5 overs and the chance to accelerate towards 300. Things happen. We were now one game (against Pakistan) away from winning the World Cup and that was my only concern.

Of all the teams I didn't want to play against in such an important fixture, it was Pakistan. Four weeks before in Adelaide we had dismissed them for 74, with Pringle and Botham almost unplayable, but rain had again interrupted and the game was abandoned. Pakistan would almost certainly not have qualified for the knockout stages had it not been for the point they gleaned from that match. From there, they really started to play some good cricket.

I tried to treat the final as any other game, although I knew that it wasn't. This could be the defining moment of a career. There was a lot of buzz around the team hotel and I knew what it meant to everyone as I had listened to so many of the other World Cup finals. To be part of an England team that finally won a World Cup would be priceless.

Going in to the match in Melbourne, I was confident that we would win the game if we played to the best of our abilities. I had known most of my teammates for a few years now and I knew the standards we could achieve as a team. Even if something was to go wrong at the start, I knew that we had enough quality throughout the group to turn things around.

We were in the field first and there I was, opening the bowling in a World Cup final – no time to savour it, just get on with it. Rameez Raja and Aamer Sohail opened for Pakistan. I ran in and bowled short and wide to Rameez, he cuts it straight to gully – no ball, the umpire calls: over shoulder height, not out. I was disappointed but there was no time to dwell, as I had to deliver the next ball. At the other end, Derek Pringle was as economical as he had been throughout the World Cup and he removed both Sohail and Raja, leaving Pakistan in some trouble on 24 for 2. This was a good start, but in at the crease now were two legends of the game in Javed Miandad and Imran Khan. I remember two moments in particular: Imran skying one to mid-wicket, and our skipper, Gooch, chasing back and diving and almost pulling off an unbelievable catch (in fact, it looked, for a while, like he had done it); and then Miandad, being hit in front twice by Pringle but given not out on both occasions. Of course, things like this happen all the time in cricket, but both batsmen were to make the most of their opportunities on this day.

The quality of both batsmen began to shine through as they found their feet. They bided their time, played themselves in and now opened up, playing their shots. Finally, a breakthrough – Javed out for 58 and then Imran for 72. But there was no respite. Inzamam-ul-Haq and Wasim Akram came in and accelerated even more, and by the end Pakistan had got to 249 for 6, 20 or 30 more than I had hoped for. That was more than we wanted to concede as a team.

For me, my 10 overs went for 52 – not great. Although I had struggled in the latter part of the tournament with that side strain, I was pain-free for the final but just didn't hit my straps. We let them get away a bit at the end, which was a little disappointing, but there were only 250 to get. We were a good batting team and it was still a good wicket to bat on. I thought we could chase that target down, but we slipped to 69 for 4 in reply. Neil Fairbrother and Allan Lamb started to turn things around with a partnership of 72 and we were now back in the game. Allan was then bowled by a wonder ball from Wasim Akram – left arm, around the wicket, pitching on off stump and hitting the top of off stump. Wow, that's always going to be difficult; I had seen Wasim up close for a while now and knew that he could produce balls like that. The quality performers know just the right time to bring out their A-games and that's what Wasim was doing. So, that ball didn't surprise me, even though it was a great delivery.

Wasim was never easy to face in any conditions, wherever you played against him. When he had the ball in his hands he could change a game in an instant. From a distance, you had to admire what he did, but not when you were 22 yards away from him. He made those facing him quake.

However, my thoughts then were not on anything other than what I was going to do – with the match still in the balance as I strode out to the middle bat in hand. In the heat of battle, I knew that I now needed to focus.

As I walked out, I was confident. I took guard and waited for Wasim; in he came. I watched the ball come out of his hand – left arm round the wicket. It was wide; it was wandering down the cut strip. I eased forward with bat aloft to let the ball go and then, suddenly, I saw it starting to tail in. I had just begun to bring my bat down, but too late. The ball glanced the face of my bat, which was still at an angle, and went into the ground, before hitting the top of leg stump.

Shit, I'm out first ball in a World Cup final. Shit. I was stuck in the crease for a few seconds, and then I realised I had to move, to drag myself off the pitch. That was the longest walk off a cricket field that I had ever experienced in my life. There were 90,000 in the ground and a worldwide audience, including all my friends and family, watching at home. I could hear my family kissing their teeth as they headed back to bed. They had probably stayed up all night to watch me play, and my innings had lasted less than thirty seconds. It's funny in such moments what your mind can come up with. I walked off the field not knowing how to react. There was nothing to say, nothing to do, and it looked like Pakistan were going to win the World Cup, pulling off an amazing smash-and-grab victory.

Throughout the whole tournament, we had played some fantastic cricket and we had just run out of steam right at the end. Without doubt, we had been a better team through the competition, but we would have to settle for the second place, in the end falling 22 runs short as we were dismissed for 227.

I watched Imran Khan and his teammates carry the trophy around the ground. We had worked so hard, and come so close, but at the end of it we had absolutely nothing. I was not enjoying this. I was quite jealous. I wanted it to be Graham Gooch lifting that trophy and the England team running around the ground parading it. I wanted it to be our team who made a nation happy that night. Losing that final, I felt like the whole few weeks in Australia – the whole winter, in fact – had been a wasted effort. We came away with nothing except a loser's medal. What ultimately had we achieved? Yes, we could say that we played in a World Cup final if we wanted to boast to someone, but in truth I was left with an overwhelming sense of disappointment. We could have – and perhaps should have – won that World Cup and then we would have been the ones walking around the Melbourne Cricket Ground (MCG) with a million cameras focused on us. We would have been the ones flying back home as heroes with memories to last us a lifetime.

There was a lot of talk in the media after the match about the two magic balls from Wasim that had turned the game around in Pakistan's favour, but to me it was just a couple of great deliveries and nothing more. I was on the balcony at Old Trafford when Shane Warne bowled what was described as 'the ball of the century'. It was a brilliant delivery, of course, and being his first in Ashes cricket match made it even more special.

Initially, that loss and my golden duck were hard for me to shake, but on the back of that there was an advert for rice, which used the footage of Wasim Akram bowling both myself and Allan Lamb. Nearly a quarter of a century later, on a visit to Pakistan, people would still recognise me from that advert. I now look back at the whole event in a more light-hearted way. Yes, it was also my only World Cup – which, of course, I didn't know at the time – but now I think of that time with pride and a smile.

Back home after the World Cup, my time at Leicester was about to come to an end. The likes of David Gower and Phillip DeFreitas had already moved on. A new three-year contract was offered to me during the summer. I had no problem signing the contract, but I did take issue with my wages as they stood at the time. I was their star name but was only on a contract worth £9,000. I was told that they didn't have any money in the coffers and so an increase for me was not possible. Nottinghamshire, meanwhile, had made an approach for my services, so I decided to leave Leicestershire, but then the chief executive at Grace Road, Mike Turner, came back with an increased offer, in fact double the amount of the initial contract, and more money than had been put on the table by Nottinghamshire. But in my mind the new deal suggested that Turner had just been taking the piss first time around and so I knew my time playing for Leicestershire was at an end.

It's always a difficult decision to move clubs. Leicestershire had been an important club for me. They had given me my start in the county game and had helped me and guided me through the works of Ken Higgs. I had some good times there. However, Nottinghamshire were a bigger club and a Test match cricket club to boot. Leicestershire on the other hand was a team in transition. They had lost some of their best players, most notably from their bowling department. They had lost Agnew, Ferris, Taylor, Clift, Parson and Benjamin; there was no longer the quality that had gone before. So much international experience had gone and now in my last summer at Grace Road I had led the attack and delivered a lot more overs. I had become a little weary of the growing expectations on my shoulders, both mentally and physically. Nottinghamshire, meanwhile, had one of the world's best all-rounders in their team in Franklyn Stephenson, who I knew I could learn from, along with Ken Higgs, also making the move to Trent Bridge as part of the coaching staff. It seemed to me that it was the obvious move to make. It was in my best interests to switch. I would be in a better place to improve my cricket. Or so I thought. Their coach, John Birch, had impressed me during our meetings – his side were winning trophies.

I would miss the friends I had made at Grace Road, the players, the office staff, the people who had taken care of me in so many ways – including paying those parking tickets! These were good people. But I was excited at the prospect of a change, to play with the likes of Chris Broad, Tim Robinson, Derek Randall, Eddie Hemmings, Chris Cairns and Bruce French – real quality performers. This was a bunch that had won trophies under Clive Rice and Richard Hadlee and had not lost that hunger to succeed and win.

I moved to Nottingham, a bigger city where there seemed to be much more to do off the field. I had heard the stories of the number of women in the city in comparison to men. It was something Nottingham was quite famous for, and I was happily looking forward to finding out myself, despite the continued rumours regarding my sexuality.

I had achieved plenty at Leicester, working my way into the first team as an 18-year-old, and eventually making my international debut, with the aid of some good people who had encouraged me and given advice. But on arriving at Trent Bridge I knew I had to prove myself all over again to my new teammates. This was a different place altogether and I knew that I had to show that I was worth my place in this team and worth the money I was now on – which still wasn't a lot. Having said that, this new kid in town was on more than many who had been playing for the county for a number of years, and I knew that this might be an issue for some. I was an outsider coming in with a contract worth £25,000 per year, which would have been a lot in comparison to some who had come through the ranks at Nottinghamshire. I knew that when it came to match time, my game face had to be on.

Before I even played my first game for Nottinghamshire, I found out that Franklyn Stephenson – a main reason for me coming to Trent bridge – had not signed a new contract and had moved on to Sussex instead. This was very disappointing. I had wanted to play in the same team as Franklyn, watch him and learn from him, as he had recently completed the amazing double of 100 first-class wickets and 1,000 first-class runs in the same season – oh well ... Then, a few months into the season, John Birch was sacked. So, the two main reasons for coming to Trent Bridge had gone. Ken Higgs was also on his way once the new coach, Alan Ormrod, came in as John's replacement. Where

Birchy seemed to have more of a hold on everything and was a good man-manager, Alan, coming in from Lancashire, appeared to have to make alliances and so the atmosphere changed. John had kept things in check, but without him things quickly deteriorated. It wouldn't work out for long.

In the dressing room, the whole experience was beginning to be a nightmare. I liked the city itself, but the environment in the dressing room with the loss of Birch was not what I had been expecting. Now, just being me seemed to be a problem. I was seen as being flash, not only for the cars I drove but for the clothes I wore. One example was the focus on my Calvin Klein underwear. 'Why did I have to wear Calvin Klein underwear? What was wrong with regular pants?' they would ask. It might seem a reasonable question but I was always taught that what other people did was none of my business. It had never occurred to me that other men would concern themselves with what underwear I was wearing.

On another occasion, I arrived at the ground, and one of the gatemen gave me a photocopy of my wage slip. He apologised, and informed me that one of my teammates had been handing it out to others around the ground. In those days, your wage slip would be left in the dressing room where you sat. One of my teammates had picked up the slip, opened it, photocopied it and handed it around the ground.

I remember playing a one-day international at Trent Bridge, as the home boy in the England team. When I walked to the crease to bat, rather than gentle applause, there was complete and utter silence. That didn't hurt, but it did tell me where I was at in my relationship with the club and its supporters.

It was a difficult dressing room, a complicated one. I remember Chris Broad being sacked. Chris was a fantastic player, he scored many hundreds for the team and he was clearly one of our best two batsmen, along with Tim Robinson. I remember being in the club offices on the morning the news came out and watching some of my fellow teammates celebrate Chris' firing. How weird. The loss of him made absolutely no sense to me.

There are so many other incidents I could mention but you get the idea.

My time at Trent Bridge was lucrative on the field, and I played some of the best county cricket of my career there, even though I was having the least amount of fun. I did well with both bat and ball – averaging 50 with the bat and 24 with the ball. Yet if you ask people, even today, how I did in my years at Nottinghamshire, they will tell you I was useless. Members of my own team wanted me to fail and that made me want to succeed even more. What the hell was it all about? It seemed to me that it was jealousy, nothing more, nothing less. From the outside looking in, these were team people and I wasn't. I soon stopped engaging with many of them.

In spite of this, the team ended up in fourth place in the County Championship. Yet, the opinion going around Trent Bridge at the time was the reason we didn't win the title was because I hadn't pulled my finger out early enough. I don't want to suggest that the problems I had fitting in were all down to everybody else. It had a lot to do with me as well; whether it was the way I behaved; that I wasn't friendly enough with either teammates or members, or that I didn't socialise enough, or maybe that I didn't kiss the right arses. To coin a phrase from another former Nottinghamshire player, it was hard being me at the time!

The likes of Hemmings, Broad, Randall, French and Robinson didn't seem to stoop so low. They were England players after all. But I don't have much else to say about a lot of that team, with the exception of Andy Afford, who was a good man. There was a lot of whispering, and in my opinion it was all to do with the fact that they were trying to hide their own performances, which weren't up to scratch. For years they had been carried by Clive Rice and Richard Hadlee and now they didn't know how to catch a cold without those two. In my time at Nottinghamshire, if we were set 300-plus in the last innings it would always take either Robinson or Broad to get 150 to lead the way. They were very impressive cricketers. The rest would already be in the committee rooms and, at times, the dressing room was a poisonous one and certainly not a place I looked forward to going in the morning.

I just got on with playing my cricket but in my second year I did not perform as well. I did make a career best of 247 against Durham, the highest individual score by a Nottinghamshire batsman since the war at the time, which was finally overtaken by Kevin Pietersen, who I bumped into once, and he was very happy to tell me about it – you may be surprised to hear that!

My third season for Nottinghamshire was the best of my career in the county game. I finished sixth in the national batting averages and was eleventh in the bowling averages. My form was good. I struck my second double hundred, an undefeated 220 against the mighty Warwickshire, who, with Brian Lara in their side, won everything that year; we were the only team to beat them that season. Brian made a duck in the second innings, bowled by his West Indian teammate, Jimmy Adams. My years at Nottingham were very productive in terms of cricket; I was almost fully grown as a player there. I was fit and strong, but little did I know that this was going be the height of my fitness.

7

ON THE UP AND THEN DOWN AGAIN

The year 1993 began with my first tour of India. The first couple of weeks in India, I was having real issues. I was in a state of shock, I had never seen anything like it – so many people living in the streets in poor conditions, seeing whole extended families begging; this had a real effect on me. It was an eye-opener. I couldn't focus, my head was everywhere; I couldn't eat. I soon became worried that, if this continued, I would be too weak to play any cricket, and that I might even be sent home. I wasn't dealing with my environment very well.

Thankfully, my appetite eventually returned, and it was on with the tour. In the end, I enjoyed playing cricket in India very much. To be honest, there wasn't much else to do apart from play cricket and practise. Not that it made any difference, as we were beaten badly over three Tests. The pitches were flat and turned, their batsmen enjoying themselves a lot: too much. But when it was our turn to bat, it was a different story altogether. Their spinners were on early, in fact sometimes even opening the bowling. It made life difficult for our batsmen.

We lost the first Test in Calcutta and the second in Madras. But Madras gave me one of my career highs: my one and only international hundred. In the first innings, I was out for a duck, a delivery from Venkatapathy Raju that turned and bounced. We followed on, and then slipped to 88 for 5 in our second innings.

It was my twenty-fifth birthday and I celebrated that milestone at one of the hotel nightclubs. The next morning I was a little tired, as you would expect, and in no mood to play around, especially after my duck in the first inning, so I decided that anything in my zone was going to go. I remember Anil Kumble tossing one up and I went after it to hit the ball over the top. Instead, it went like a rocket along the ground. I was away, riding my luck in the beginning, but soon, timing pretty much everything. Shortly before the close of play, I moved into the 90s, I asked myself how I was now going to approach things: singles to get the job done was one school of thought, but another voice was saying, 'No, you've got this far playing this way so just carry on'.

Raju was bowling (or was it Rajesh Chauhan, I can't remember). I came down the pitch unsure of what I was going to do – a bit of a fishing expedition – but I was there: close enough to the pitch, so I went with it. I played the shot and the ball flew over the boundary for 6. My first feeling was just of joy, well a lot of joy, and then a little bit of pride. It was a big relief to know that I could score a Test hundred, was this really happening? My first Test hundred, wow! It took a while for it to sink in, but I loved that feeling.

We lost that second Test match, and the third and final one in Mumbai, where I scored runs again, but nowhere near as many as Vinod Kambli, who batted for more than ten hours to make a double century. I stood at first slip for a lot of that innings and I knew he didn't fancy short-pitch bowling. But on those flat pitches he could ease onto the front foot and drive time and time again. It pissed me off, if I'm honest. I tried to be as fast and hostile as I could at him, but still to no avail.

I grew up listening to Sunil Gavaskar scoring double hundreds against the West Indies, and throughout the years India have produced some of the most fantastic batsmen in world cricket. But, no one was as good as the amazing Sachin Tendulkar. He oozed class, and for a young man on this tour, he didn't seem to have an obvious weakness. He perfectly complemented Mohammed Azharuddin and Navjot Sidhu, the axe man, who seemed to like nothing more than charging down the wicket and hitting our spinners out of the ground. India had a formidable batting line-up and too often they would post a large first inning scores and then get their spinners to work: the ball turning and bouncing straight away. It was hard work for our batsmen. It wasn't easy work for the bowlers either.

Off the field, I enjoyed my three months in India. So much of it reminded me of home. The food, the smells, the colours, the people ... remember, Guyana has a very large Indian population.

And without a doubt, cricket is number one for their people. They have so much passion for the game, it was a real joyful experience being in some of the grounds and witnessing the atmosphere. It was loud, and every ground was packed to the rafters. India was just as I had imagined it back when I was a young boy listening to cricket on the radio back in Guyana – full of life, colour and passion.

On my return to England, I was chosen as England's International Cricketer of the Year; an award I shared with Alec Stewart. Back home it was February, no cricket for months. One day, I was hanging out with my manager, Gareth James, thinking about things to do that would be fun. Gareth had various companies asking if I was available to do different kinds of work. One offer seemed to be just the sort of fun we were looking for: a request to get my kit off, posing for a ladies' magazine called *For Women* – only down to my jockstrap. This sounded like a blast, and so the plans were made and soon off we went to the studio in London.

I had worked out hard before going to India, knowing that I needed to be in good shape. I thought my body looked good, but I had become a little body conscious. We started to take some shots; initially, they were of me in my cricket whites. Then it was down to my jock strap: spilling milk on my chest. Later in the afternoon we were running out of things to do, so we decided that it would be a good idea to take some snaps with a model pouring the milk down my chest, just to see if the pictures looked better. I don't know about looking better, but it sounded a whole lot better. Later, a model turned up and we took a few shots to see how they looked with the two of us together: no, no, too much like porn. So we decided to stick with the ones we had taken earlier in the day, with me on my own. But all in all, I had a lovely day. I wasn't bored for a second of it, and it wasn't over yet; we ended the evening at the photographer's party filled, of course, with lots of beautiful women: life can be good. As far as I was concerned, I had a great evening and that was the end of it. I was asked if I wanted to see the shots, but I didn't have any interest. I had simply had a day of fun on my down time. I then got back down to training and practice. I even forgot that I had taken those pictures.

Months passed. On the morning of the second Test at Lord's, against the Australians – during the Ashes, no less – out came the pictures. I didn't expect that: where did they come from? This was perfect timing for the magazine, of course, but not for me. The perception was that just days before a Test match – an *Ashes* Test match – I had been posing for half-naked shots in a magazine and not focusing on my job, which was to play cricket for England and beat Australia (bearing in mind that we had just lost the first Test very heavily, and there was a lot of excitement in the papers about Shane Warne's wonder ball at Old Trafford). Yet, as you now know, those pictures had been taken two or three months before. Still, all hell broke loose.

The next five days of this match were going to be hard work. There was a furore around the members at Lord's – cricketers don't do that sort of thing, stripping for magazines – while the media were having a lot of fun with this story. There was chatter at the Home of Cricket as to what cricketers should or should not do, and the general view from Lord's, as was often the case, was that this 'just wasn't cricket, old boy'. I was almost used to that kind of reaction by now, but I suppose I wasn't a traditional type of guy.

But back to the cricket. As a team, we were in big trouble on the pitch. Australia's top three batsmen all made hundreds, and numbers 4 and 5 were not far away either – the tourists made 632 for 4, with my contribution being 2 for 151. Things didn't get any better with a bat in hand either; in fact, it got worse. I went out to bat, with us on 131 for 5 in reply and only Michael Atherton surviving for any length of time. The Aussies were waiting for me, and they were not going to miss their chance of taking the piss: 'Here comes the stripper!' I tried not to laugh, but I did find it funny. Right, concentrate. I could feel the eyes of the ground looking my way: those magazines pictures seemed to be everywhere. Within minutes, Shane Warne had trapped me in front for a duck. The walk back to the pavilion was a quiet and lonely one; you could cut the atmosphere with a knife – the same knife that some would later like to stick in my back. We followed on, a long way behind, and with awful timing, I was out for a duck again in the second innings – stumped. Wandering down the wicket aimlessly, I had myself a pair, my first in international cricket. I could not have picked a worse moment to get a pair. Not good timing. If you are going to do things like clubbing and posing half-naked in magazines, you'd better make sure you perform on the field; that's your only chance, but I'd got a pair and gone for 150. This was a challenging moment in my life. Just a few Test matches ago, I was the Player of the Year and just two Tests into the summer, I'm not sure if I can hold a bat. Before the third Test, Graham Gooch (England captain at the time) telephoned to tell me that I had been dropped for the next test: my professionalism, or rather lack of it, being brought into question.

I had no problem with the decision to drop me based on my performance. That was fair enough; I hadn't performed anywhere near my best. Nor had anyone else, for that matter. We had lost by an innings and plenty. But I was only concerned with my own efforts: not good enough. Today, I remember that photo shoot with fondness. There was no cricket in sight and I had a blast. As I sit here, I can smile about the whole episode as it added a bit of colour to life, but at the time, after that Test match, I couldn't see the funny side.

It was back to county cricket, playing in a second team. I wasn't in form and needed practice, and playing as much cricket as possible seemed to be the best way to go about things; my international summer was over. Soon, however, I was back with England in the Caribbean at the start of 1994, and I plunged myself into even more controversy. I became known as 'The Prat Without a Hat' by *The Sun* newspaper – this was after I shaved my head and then went down with sunstroke. The truth of the story is slightly different to how it was reported, so here goes.

My brother Mark and I had decided earlier in the winter to shave our heads for charity. But it was winter, so I didn't want to run the risk of catching a cold or even the flu. This was young Chris, trying to be 'professional'. So I decided I would wait till I got out to the warmth of the Caribbean: no chance of catching the flu out there. On the first day after arriving in Antigua I got to it: shaving my head clean. It looked great; I proudly showed it off at breakfast to everyone and went about my business. A couple of days later I didn't feel that well. I had caught sunstroke. It never occurred to me that I could even get sunstroke, but I laugh about it now, of course. After all, my head had never been bald before and placing it in the midday sun – a Caribbean sun, which I hadn't seen for many years – was bound to cause problems.

It all went pear-shaped and I was hammered for getting sunstroke and missing one of our warm-up games. *The Guardian* newspaper reported: 'Only mad dogs, Englishmen and opening batsmen go out in the midday sun here. Yesterday the dogs and batsmen were perfectly happy, but Englishman Lewis was in the doghouse back in his hotel room.' The media had a field day. Not helped by the tour manager telling the press, when asked why I wasn't playing in the first practice game, that 'Chris has fried brains'. Thus I became 'The Prat Without a Hat'. There was someone who kept faxing all the newspaper headlines from England to me at the hotel in Antigua: I think one of the papers called me some sort of vegetable head; they were giving out Chris Lewis sunblock packs. It took me a while to find the funny side of things, but in retrospect I can see that it was comical. This was the tour that saw Brian Lara break Gary Sobers' longstanding individual world record of 365 as the highest innings in Test match history. Little Brian was something else, what a player, his 375 in Antigua in the last game of the series made headlines all around the world. However, I did not ever think that I would be playing in a match where one batsman scored that many runs, and that Gary Sobers' record would be broken.

It is, of course, a very famous moment in cricket – repeated on TV over and over again – but over the years, because I bowled that delivery, I have felt like some people think that he got all 375 of my bowling, which has become a bit of a pain. I still cannot pass the local West Indian food shop without someone shouting 'Lara!' I have seen that picture of him pulling that ball to the fence so many times, but here is something that not many people know: that when Brian hooked that ball for 4, he actually stepped on his stumps. There is a photograph of Brian stepping on the stumps, with the bails up in the air and then falling back into the groove. I could have become the man who denied Brian his moment in the sun – well, his first anyway. He's had a lot of moments in the sun. At the time, in the midst of the battle, I would have loved that, but not now. These days, I embrace history like everybody else.

The pitch was a flat one, but who would have ever imagined that a batsman was going to break the world record, one which had stood since 1958. It just seemed to unfold. Lara was different to anyone I had ever played with or against. Nobody had his ability to score big runs, massive runs. Lots of batsmen made sizeable hundreds, but Brian, once in, had an appetite like no other. He took the game away from you, quickly, single-handedly. What a player, the hardest of batsmen to bowl to.

What cricket stats don't tell us is that, in fact, I had already broken Sobers' record – in my back garden as a young boy. It took me two days because I had to go inside for my dinner and to school, but I ran every run, and played all the shots, bouncing the ball off the wall in the back garden.

It was an awesome feat by Brian, but there was zero enjoyment while he was doing it. We had taken a couple of early wickets but, aside from that, it was a game to be forgotten. My undefeated 75 rightly went unnoticed by everyone else but me. The pitch was so batsman-friendly, I was able to pull Curtly Ambrose to the boundary: in front of square and then dare to stare back at him. He was a man you really did not want to make eye contact with. As easy-paced as the pitch was, you could still never take anything away from what Lara achieved there. It was an absolutely monumental effort.

It was the start of 1995 season. Having missed out on the tour to Australia in the winter, I was not in the Test team, but being rested and trained I was ready for the new season. I felt physically strong and fit. Right at the beginning of the season, I remember bowling to Roger Twose in a Benson & Hedges Cup game against Warwickshire at Trent Bridge. Roger was a pain in the arse, as he tended to hit the ball into some unusual areas. I was trying hard to get him out: a lot of effort. I let one delivery go at him and felt a clicking in my hips as I followed through. This was unusual; I had never felt it before. I knew straight away that it wasn't muscles; it felt like something deeper. I kept on bowling without much discomfort, and we went on to win the match.

The games came thick and fast this time of year, and a couple of days later we were in Leek taking on the Minor Counties. I bowled my first spell of six overs without any problems, but the second spell would be very different: after just a few deliveries I was in a lot of pain, shooting straight down my leg, and it was getting worse by the end of the over. I had no strength in my leg. This wasn't normal. It felt like an electrical signal pulsating right through my leg: from my hip joint, straight down to my toes. I couldn't put any pressure on it. I left the field but it got even worse, and by the end of the day I was unable to walk. My teammate Andy Afford had to drive me home.

This was the beginning of a very long haul, the beginning of a hip injury that would last until the present day. I had lots of tests, saw lots of specialists and in the end I was diagnosed with avascular necrosis, which essentially means that a part of my hip joint had died; there was no blood flow and the material in between my hip joint seemed to be non-existent. Therefore, there was no level of protection to the hip joint. It was bone on bone, especially when I was banging my feet down during my delivery stride.

At this time, I felt there was a lack of understanding regarding the injury by those at Nottinghamshire, once again some believing that I might even be faking it because I didn't want to play. Heaven only knows why. I just had to rest and hope that things would get better quickly. After many weeks, it became apparent that this was going to be a long-term injury. The rest of the summer was going to be a write-off and one thought was that it could be the end of my cricket career. Aside from having a hip replacement, there didn't seem to be any other options available. But people who were having hip replacements couldn't play professional cricket, so it wasn't going to be for me: I still wanted to play cricket.

One day, while at Trent Bridge being assessed and receiving treatment for my injury, I was called into the club office. I was told that if I wanted to leave the club then I could: that's a strange one, wanting to leave when I could not play and was not even sure whether I could play again? Rubbish, I hadn't asked to leave, where had that come from? If I wanted to leave, I was told, my salary would not be paid, and I had to make a decision within a couple of hours – not days but hours. My time at Nottinghamshire had been an unpleasant one. Feeling pissed off and angry, I left the ground to ponder my future. In my time with Nottinghamshire, had I not put my body on the line for the club? Proof of which, here I stand: injured playing for them and not sure what was going to happen next. I just became angrier and angrier as I thought about the whole situation. What had just happened? A couple of hours later I was headed back to the ground, steaming: what a cheeky bunch of so and sos. Had I not played cricket for Notts, played it well and, whilst doing so, had to put up with their abuse? But now I was injured they want me to fuck off without paying me! I told them that I wanted to leave, didn't want to be there at any price.

I have heard many times from people over the years that when it was announced over the tannoy that my time at Nottinghamshire was at an end there was a cheer from the spectators. If there was cheering, it would simply fit in with my whole experience of the place. I wasn't amongst friends in Nottingham. That was made clear by the fact that, if the rumours were true, the members were applauding the loss of an all-rounder who averaged more than the leading batters, took more wickets than anyone else and was most probably the leading catcher. I think that said more about them and the county at the time than it did about me. They did the same with Chris Broad.

The whole experience in Nottingham was a very forgettable one. I just never felt part of the club. A week later I was back at Trent Bridge to clear out my locker – but there was nothing there to clear out. My locker had been opened and a lot of my England kit, sweaters, caps and so on, had all gone missing. I did enquire about what had happened to my stuff but nobody seemed to know anything. Later, I was told by a teammate that two of my colleagues had opened my locker and taken my things so they could use it for their benefits, which were coming up in the following year. What a cheek! With all that had gone on before, why did they think it was OK to do that? Of course, nothing was done about it.

I left Trent Bridge with no further prospect of a wage for that year, still badly injured and not knowing whether I would play again. But I was pleased to have left. Trent Bridge for me at that time was a place where lots of people made their livings in the committee rooms rather than on the cricket field. How long you lasted was more dependent on the conversations you had with your allies in those committee rooms rather than your performances on the cricket field. There were some who did nothing other than talk behind the backs of their teammates. I, of course, was oblivious to all of this; I hadn't realised that this was part of the game at this time. I simply thought the best way forward was to play cricket. In hindsight, this seems naïve. I didn't think that in order to keep my job, I had to get others sacked.

I left Trent Bridge and drove home. Only a few hours before I had a contract and a certain amount of security. Now what was I going to do? In no time at all, my mind came up with the answer. I didn't care what the diagnosis was. I was going to carry on playing cricket. I had to. For the rest of the summer I was left to my own devices. This was the time that I started to go out a lot more, even drinking and smoking. The smoking was new; I had never smoked before, but here I was trying weed for the first time. Would I say I got into the wrong crowd? No, just too much time on my hands. My friends had been my friends for a long time and I had never felt any pressure to smoke with them before. Ian, a friend from school, tried to dissuade me, but no, I was going to try it: another poor choice.

During the winter, my leg improved; I still couldn't bowl but the pain wasn't as bad. At least I could start going to the gym. I needed to be fitter, I needed to be stronger. I needed to be strong enough so my hips and legs didn't hurt so much. It was perfect timing then when a friend introduced me to a fitness instructor called Kwame. His thing was 'Afrobics' – aerobics to African music. He was fit, and knew his stuff. He could run forever. We would train hard during the days and then go clubbing at night, then straight afterwards, he would go running. Kwame would become my brother. He knew the challenges ahead and started to get me ready for them. No mucking around here, just the running and Kwame screaming.

In the early part of 1996 I was contacted by an old England teammate, Alec Stewart, who wanted me at the Oval, but was told that I would have to prove my fitness during pre-season in order to get a contract. Back in London, I trained even harder with my fitness test to come in April. It was great to be back in the city where I was brought up; I knew London. I seemed to fit right in there. I could just get lost in it and the city seemed to be more accepting of me, which had not always been the case in the East Midlands.

Winter turned to spring and I was at the Oval. It was time for pre-season with Surrey. I was not in a bad place, but I was not in a great one either. I had become a lot stronger. I had bulked up and was feeling a lot better, but there was still an issue. When I bowled a spell my leg felt fine, but once I had finished my leg would stiffen up and become weak, and that shooting pain would be back as well. As long as I kept moving, it didn't work too badly. But as soon as I stopped, it would stiffen up: 20 overs today would mean three or four days of pain and stiffness before I was ready to bowl again. Sometimes it took half an hour to get out of bed. I would wake with shooting pains in my legs and back first thing in the morning, not knowing if the pain and stiffness would ease enough for me to bowl. Practice became difficult. If I practised too hard then I wouldn't be fit enough for a game. There was only so much I could do before the hip and my leg would give way under the constant grinding of bone on bone.

Nevertheless, by the end of April I had a two-year contract with Surrey and my new employers were happy. A huge weight had been lifted off my shoulders. But this situation would take some managing.

My new teammates were as far removed from my old ones at Trent Bridge as possible. Surrey pretty much had a team of internationals, with the likes of Mark Butcher, Adam Hollioake, Graham Thorpe, Martin Bicknell, Brendon Julian, Alec Stewart and Ali Brown. All of these guys seemed to have interests of their own. Nobody was at all interested in what I was doing or what I was wearing, whether I had an earring or a Mercedes. After the experience at Trent Bridge, this was brilliant. As captain, Adam Hollioake was only interested in performances on the field – a simple approach that I supported wholeheartedly.

I enjoyed the company of my new teammates at Surrey. They had attitude, and I enjoyed the Surrey crowd. I realised that perhaps I was more of a Londoner than I had thought before. They called those who played for the county 'Surrey Swaggers' and that fitted in with me fine. I loved being there and it was no surprise to me that we won trophies, claiming the Sunday League in our first year, beating Nottinghamshire on run rate alone, and the Benson & Hedges Cup in my second season at the club. This was the happiest I had been on a cricket field since my childhood.

The summer of 1996 began well for me. I was back in the England one-day side after a year out of the game, the move to Surrey having given me just what I needed at that time. I had proven my fitness and had done enough to warrant a place in the national team for the series with India. I was over the moon. It had been a difficult year, but now things seemed to be going in the right direction.

The first ODI at the Oval went well. I remember thinking during the game, 'wow, I never thought I'd play for Engalnd again!' At that moment, I felt so blessed. I hurled myself at the batsmen, bowling as fast as I could. There was pent-up frustration, of course, but overall I was just happy to be part of the England team again. I took 4 for 40 on my return, in a match that was eventually rained off with us well on top. We won the remaining two games: I was named as England's Man of the Series. Yes, get in there!

I was then selected for the first Test match against the same opposition at Edgbaston. After Nasser Hussain had set up the game nicely with a big hundred, I took 5 for 72 in the second innings to help us win by 8 wickets, the other two games being drawn. It was a series I remember particularly well for the Test debuts of Saurav Ganguly and Rahul Dravid. Although you could see the class in both players, I never would have imagined that they would go on and achieve what they did in their fantastic international careers.

Meanwhile, I had settled in as England's opening bowler, back to my best both on and off the field. After the problems at Nottinghamshire and my injury worries, life was going well again. Being back in the England fold was great, and I was perhaps at my most comfortable within it. I was not a young man anymore and had been around the team, on and off, for a while. I was also playing against some opposition who had less experience than I did, and I felt I could take advantage of their inexperience. An illness meant I missed the first Test of the following series later that summer against Pakistan, but I was back for the second Test, where I shared the new ball with my former Leicestershire teammate Alan Mullally, before heading to the Oval for the last match of the season, with us trailing in the rubber 1–0. Everything was still to play for.

It was Saturday. We were three days into the Test match at the Oval against Pakistan, in the final game of the summer; we were struggling to keep in touch with our opponents. I was informed there was going to be a team photo on Sunday morning, and I would need my England blazer. I didn't have mine with me as we had been allowed to wear suit and ties for the Test. 'Not to worry, manager,' I said to David Lloyd. 'I live only 15 minutes from the ground, so I will go home and get my blazer at the end of the day's play.' So, as promised, at the end of play, I drove home to get the blazer. Once there, my own bed looked so inviting that I decided to stay the night and head back to the ground in the morning. I'm closer to the ground anyway.

It was two o'clock in the morning and I was wide awake. I tossed and turned for a while, then came up with a gem, or so I thought. I would call a friend who lived in Streatham, even closer to the ground. I drove over. Let's just say that we sat up and talked for a while, and then at last it was time to sleep. Ever the professional, I set the alarm for 8 a.m. I had to be at the Oval for 9.

I was still half asleep when I felt the sun coming through the window. This was not an eight o'clock sun. My brain suddenly clicked in. I looked over at the alarm clock – ten o'clock! Fuck! Fuck, fuck, fuck, I was supposed to have been at the ground an hour ago. The boys would already be on the field preparing for the day's play. I jumped into my clothes – socks, shoes, all at once, and I was out the door in a flash, heading down Streatham Hill. Not for the first time in my career, I was soon on the phone to my manager, Gareth. 'What's up?' he asked. I replied, 'There's just one thing you need to know and that is I am not at the ground yet.' That's all I had to say to him. I was never flavour of the month in some quarters, and now I'd served my head on a silver platter. We both knew that this wasn't going to have a happy ending.

I got to the Oval and, as expected, all hell had broken loose. I soon discovered that Ray Illingworth, the supremo of English cricket, had been on the TV announcing the one-day squad and pointing out that I was late at the ground. What was I going to do with this one? What was I going to say to everyone? Holy shit – a puncture, that was it, that's what I was going to say. I knew it wasn't much of an excuse, but it was the best I could come up with at such short notice. I hadn't thought about what to say while driving to the ground, my mind had been going everywhere. I was called in to a private room; the captain Michael Atherton and coach David Lloyd of course wanted to know what had gone on. I knew that I had let them down and all my teammates as well. But especially Athers. I was aware that he had supported me many times before by giving me opportunities when others were prepared to turn their backs on me. I had much to be thankful to him for. I told them that I had a puncture, but they were not having it. Then, they inquired, why had I not called to tell them what was going on? Oh no, here comes another lie: 'My phone had run out of charge,' I blurted out. But in reality I could hardly have called, as I had been still asleep.

It was an awful morning, embarrassing. What a mess. I had been playing good cricket. Now I had not just shot myself in the foot, but in both feet at once.

The reaction in the dressing room was as expected: the odd cheeky comment, but I could feel the tension. I had just let them down. We were a team and this was a Test match, an important one. For me not to be there on time, missing practice and the warm-up with my colleagues, was certainly letting everyone down – the whole team and the nation at large. I got myself together and prepared for the day's play – all eyes would be on me again.

We went onto the field and Pakistan's batsman Asif Mujtaba soon dabbed one down to third man, where I had been placed out of the way – sent to Coventry as it were. He hadn't got the longest legs, nor was he the fastest runner, but for some reason he decided to take me on, trying to pinch a second run. I picked up the ball one-handed, and hurled it into the gloves of wicket keeper Alec Stewart, right over the stumps. I couldn't have sent in a better throw if I had tried it 100 times over. Mujtaba was run out and we had the early breakthrough that we so badly needed. I celebrated with Stewy and Athers, who both reacted very differently, Alec jovial and Mike still with a disappointed look on his face. Rightly, nobody ever believed my story about a puncture or that my mobile phone, one we had all been given by a sponsor, had run out of battery. I had to say something; I think that all the players knew what I was really up to. Incidentally, I never brought my blazer to the ground.

Do I relive those moments in my mind from time to time? Of course I do, but once things are done, they are done; you can't unring the bell. I was dropped by England and wasn't included in the winter tour. My Test career was over. That would be my last Test match for England. I played some good cricket that summer.

It was back to Surrey, where I learnt that someone from the English Cricket Board (ECB) had called the club and tried to get me dropped by Surrey as well as England. Surrey were having none of it; as far as my coach at Surrey, Dave Gilbert, was concerned, being dropped by England was punishment enough for me. They even made me captain in the absence of Adam Hollioake: it was a nice feeling being backed by the club at this time. Surrey won the Sunday League, coming out of nowhere and taking everyone by surprise. We were third or fourth in the table as we took on Northamptonshire at the Oval in our penultimate game. They were above us in the table. We sneaked past them to win by 2 wickets off the last ball, my 63 helping us along the way and Martin Bicknell finishing the game off.

We then headed to Cardiff to take on Glamorgan, knowing that a victory there would give us the title. We bowled tightly and reduced the Welshmen to 159 for 9 from their 40 overs. Adam Hollioake, who had a fantastic competition with the ball, once again led the way in the field. We then chased the total down comfortably, winning by 7 wickets with 7 overs to spare. It was fantastic to be part of a trophy-winning team. I had seen so many pictures over the years of players celebrating after winning tournaments and at last I could do the same. And there were more celebrations to come.

Patricia and a young Chris, recently arrived from Guyana.

Chris with younger sister Vanessa.

Home away from home: Mum, cousin Dinah, Chris, Gran and Auntie Hazel.

Chris just chillaxing.

Chris, still the schoolboy, with younger brother Mark.

Chris with baby brother Mikhail.

Back in Guyana with family.

Joining Leicestershire for the second time.

At a press conference.

Above and below: My home when it comes to cricket; the Oval, with the fans.

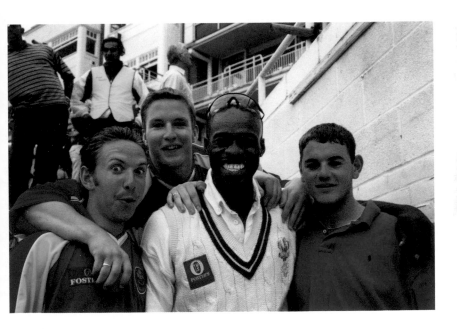

Doing this job can't be difficult.

Winning in Barbados – priceless.

Chris right in the thick of the action.

Touring in New Zealand with the boys; this was the beginning of Twenty20.

Sometimes you rise only to fall.

Chris doing what counts the most: inspiring the next generation.

Young and without a care in the world.

Chris Lewis in illustrious company, including John Major and Nelson Mandela.

The 1997 Benson & Hedges Cup final was a day I will always remember. We had lost only one game in the competition, that being against Kent at the Oval, and they were now our opponents in the final again. We were going to have to be at our best to beat them.

I opened the bowling to Matthew Fleming and Matt Walker. My first over was expensive; going for double figures (I think it was 13) I headed back to third man with my tail between my legs. 'If the rest of my overs go like this, it's going to be a very long day for me,' I thought. It was my first Lord's final; this wasn't a good start! The only thing to do as I began my second over was to run in hard and bowl fast: be aggressive, meet fire with fire. I charged in first ball, it nipped back down the hill and caught Fleming on the crease in two minds. I went up for the appeal, more in hope than expectation, but the umpire's finger was raised. Surprised, we were off and running.

Alan Wells was the next man in my sights, and as I bowled to him the momentum of my follow-through kept taking me right down the pitch. I was not in a playful mood and I stared hard at Alan, making sure he knew that I had my game face on. I was not a man for sledging too much, but on this occasion, I was trying to distract the batsmen, getting them to think about something else while I was trying to get through a few overs. I followed my wicket with two more maidens, while at the other end, Martin Bicknell did what Martin Bicknell always did, which was to give nothing away.

We soon had Kent in trouble. I came back on for a second spell, ending with figures of 3 for 39 from my 10 overs, as Kent struggled to a total of 212 for 9 from their 50. It was now our turn to bat, with me down to come in at number 6. I sat on the balcony feeling more nervous than ever. I couldn't watch, so went to the nets to hit a few balls, I was desperate to win – as we all were, of course. Even though we had bowled well on a fairly flat pitch, as in all one-day games, anything was still possible. We lost Ali Brown early to a stunning one-handed catch by Fleming at gulley, but all that did was bring in young Ben Hollioake, who played an innings as only Ben could – with class, skill and carefreeness. It was his day, as he struck a brilliant 98.

In the dressing room we remained focused until the winning run was struck. We won the game comfortably, by 8 wickets with 5 overs to spare. I was euphoric, as was the whole of the team. Finally playing and winning in a Lord's final was a great experience. My two younger brothers, Mark and Mikhail, were at the game so I asked our captain, Adam Hollioake, if I could invite them up into the dressing room to sample the atmosphere. He agreed, and I will never forget my two young brothers sitting quietly, soaking it all up, while we drank champagne and behaved like children. It was going to be a long night. We were staying in a hotel just down the road from Lord's in Swiss Cottage, and about seven or eight of the guys jumped into my convertible car with the trophy. It was like a mini parade down the street, through St John's Wood. We had won, and it was time to party. We had a big night at Café de Paris. This was what cricket was all about, playing your best, winning trophies and celebrating with friends afterwards.

We celebrated long and hard. I think I drank Jack Daniels. It didn't taste very nice, but it caused me the least amount of stress to get down. Afterwards I was described in one of the newspapers as a Chicago gangster for the way I had behaved towards the batsmen that day – aggressively. To me, this was just typical; anybody else would be seen to have been showing heart or passion, but I was being a gangster. People have their opinions, of course. I would like to offer my opinion, too. Journalists knew that I was an easy target. They could kick and not get anything back in return. They just delivered some cheap shots, and it was all rather pointless and nasty: always flippant. While I certainly hadn't helped myself over the years, I did find that the media overall created the version of me that they were most happy with.

That aside, my two years at Surrey were the most enjoyable time of my cricket career. I learned a lot whilst I was there, mostly that cricket could be fun and enjoyable, just the way it was when I was growing up. It was not so much learning as remembering to just have fun. Adam Hollioake told me when I arrived at the Oval that he was only interested in my performance on the field and in my two years there we never had a cross word. It was the way I imagined cricket would be played – go to work, do your job and then get on with the rest of your life.

Surrey's players rose above all the tittle-tattle that could be found in other dressing rooms where less talented players sat. They got on with what they were being paid to do, rather than bickering and moaning, whispering and gossiping. They had confidence. The crowd at the Oval were also fantastic. I remember dropping a catch on the boundary in a Sunday League game and the supporters applauded – not sarcastically, but to encourage me, to lift me back up. I can't think of a single bad memory from my time in south London. We had fun on the field and we had fun off it. My partner in crime was Ben Hollioake. In spite of our age gap, we got on immediately. We would take the piss out of one another constantly. His name

131

for me was Big Dog, and mine for him was Small Dog. He was a brilliant young player. He was confident, cheeky and had an enormous amount of ability. He was also probably the only person I had ever met who I never heard a bad word spoken about. He never seemed to put anybody's nose out of joint. He had a talent for being likeable, which is something I admired him for. I thought we would be friends for a long time but, of course, that was not to be. His life was tragically brought to an end at the age of only 24 when he died in a car crash in Perth.

I was in bed in Nottingham when I heard the news of Ben's death. It was hard to understand. It had happened before during my first spell at Leicestershire; a young teammate called Richard Edmunds had died in a car crash. He was a very good left-arm pace bowler with good prospects of playing for England in the future. We finished training one day and when I got home I received the news that he was in a coma. He was on his way home and was involved in a head-on collision – there one minute and then gone the next. It took a while for that to sink in; it seemed unfathomable. In Richard's case, I had only seen him a couple of hours before. In both cases, I was left numb with many questions left unanswered.

8

THE DOWNWARD SPIRAL

At the end of my second summer with Surrey in 1997, I received a call from someone I had known for years, a man from Leicestershire called Roger Goadby, who ran a hosiery company but was now the chairman of the county. I had also represented his company in six-aside cricket competitions many years ago in my first spell with Leicester. Roger was offering me an opportunity to return to Grace Road as vice-captain, and when James Whitaker moved on I would take over as the county captain. This was about the only offer that would have taken me away from the Oval. The idea of captaining a county side was a dream that I had yet to fulfil. I had skippered as a replacement at Surrey and felt very capable of doing the job, but when it came to the important games and cup finals I was not going to be the one who lifted the trophy. Adam Hollioake had the role at Surrey. He was much younger than I was, and was going to be doing that job for some time. And so, with some regret, I decided to make the move back to Leicester, the plan being to tick the final box of being a county captain.

Leaving Surrey was emotional. In an ideal world, I would have stayed longer, to see out my career there. But the prospect of finally being a captain of a county side was one I could not let pass me by. I had always wanted to do that job and had always hoped that one day I would be given an opportunity. I was excited about this new challenge, one that I thought might just show what I was capable of. I had been playing cricket for a long time now and knew that I had the skill and knowhow to do the job.

It had been five years since I left Leicester and the club had changed, but there were some players and staff who remained, enough familiar faces who made bedding in a little bit easier. Our first championship game of the season was at home to Worcestershire, and our club captain, James Whitaker, was injured and likely to be out for some time. This was the chance to grab the bull by the horns, as the saying goes. The first three days were rained off but I used nine bowlers and I only had 5 overs, from which I grabbed a couple of wickets.

We played some decent cricket from the start. In Bristol we defeated Gloucestershire before sticking around the top of the championship table for the first half of the campaign. The season really picked up, though, in mid-July, when we took on Northamptonshire at home. It looked as if the match was heading for a draw after Graeme Swann, who had never made a first-class 50 before, struck 92 in the first innings and 111 in the second. This left us with 20 overs in the game's final hour to get 204 to win.

We had bowled poorly on the last day, but there was nothing to lose. I asked Vinny Wells to take on the bowling from the off, and that he did. After just a few overs we had 50 on the board and were in with a shout, even though Northants had a good attack, including Devon Malcolm, Franklyn Rose and Paul Taylor and Graeme Swann. Given our approach, wickets inevitably fell and I went into bat with still a bit to do. I came in with the total of 99 for 3 and initially tried to hit the ball out of the park, with no success.

Then Taylor, bowling left arm over, dropped one on leg stump and my natural swing caught up with the ball. I middled it, and it went miles. Suddenly, I was away. By the time we got to the game's last over, we needed 4 to win. I hit Franklyn Rose's first ball to the boundary. Incredible; we had won! We made 204 for 6 in 19.1 overs in a championship game with no field restrictions and I had played my part, finishing on 71 from 32 balls.

It was a brilliant team effort. Those sorts of things were unheard of back then, before the age of Twenty20 cricket. The atmosphere in the dressing room was fantastic. From being on a downer just a couple of hours before, looking like we were missing out on points which would have kept us in the title race, we had pulled off an improbable victory.

From there the season really took off. As a club, we really hit our straps and everybody played their part with runs and wickets just when they were needed. But then, yet more trouble for yours truly as I lost the captaincy in late August to Phil Simmons.

We were playing against Nottinghamshire at Worksop, not a million miles away from Leicester, where I was living at the time. The day before the game we were to have a training session at the ground in Worksop. 'Don't be late tomorrow, Lewy', manager Jack Birkenshaw told me – but I ended up driving in to the ground just as the guys were coming out to practise. I was dropped from the team and had the captaincy removed from me. I did not take this very well. I was angry – mostly with myself. Our coach, Jack Birkenshaw, had told me not to be late. I had blown it, and had no excuses. I should have just set off to the ground half an hour sooner, rather than cutting it so fine, and it wasn't the first time that I had done this; my timekeeping was never particularly good. I always tried to get to somewhere on time, but never early. However, I thought the punishment was severe and did not fit the crime. I had been handling the captaincy well and the bosses had thought so, too. Without me, Phil Simmons and Ben Smith both scored big, and we hammered Nottinghamshire by an innings and plenty.

The championship title was going to be decided in the very last week of the summer. The guys at Surrey were a few points ahead of us, but we headed south to meet them at the Oval knowing that if we could beat them the title was Leicestershire's for the second time in three years. It would be my first. Despite the quality of players at Surrey's disposal, I knew we had a good chance. We were a side with form and were filled with confidence. That was in evidence when Ben Smith struck his maiden double hundred, while Aftab Habib and Paul Nixon hit a hundred each. I was at the crease on 54 when we declared on a massive 585 for 6. Then, everyone who was asked to bowl bowled like a demon. Alan Mullally and David Millns both took early wickets, which had Surrey on 0 for 3 and then 8 for 4. We were on a roll; they never recovered. They were dismissed for 146 and, following on, were bowled out again for 228 as we took the game by an innings and 211 runs with a day to spare. We had won the championship. After a long summer of cricket, to end up on top was priceless.

I sat and watched James Whitaker and Phil Simmons lift the trophy with a heavy heart, knowing that I had skippered the club in more than half the games we played. Before I lost the job, we had competed well in all competitions. We finished fourth in the Sunday League, lost by only 3 runs to Derbyshire in the NatWest Bank Trophy semi-final and were beaten finalists in the Benson and Hedges Cup. It was arguably the best season Leicestershire had ever had.

The final against Essex was a major disappointment, though. It was not a good match for me in many ways. Here I was, captaining my county in a Lord's final, and that felt great. Things had gone well throughout the competition. We had lost the first match of the tournament to Lancashire but had won all the others very comfortably, the best being a 20-run success in the semi-final against Surrey at Grace Road in what was a very high-scoring game. We were favourites to win the final.

It was an overcast day in mid-July and I knew that the ball would do something first thing. The plans had been set; the same ones that had seen us perform so brilliantly to get us to the Home of Cricket. I won the toss and inserted the opposition, Alan Mullally and I opened the bowling – the aim being to stifle the Essex openers while making the most of some dampness in the pitch. Early wickets, and we would be on our way. As we walked through the famous Long Room and then came down the pavilion steps, Al was at me about bowling from the Pavilion End. All year, I hadn't given Mullally the choice of ends. One of the reasons for that is he bowled at only about 75mph and so I would generally have him bowling into the wind. He liked to moan about it from time to time, but he got on with the job and did it well. But this time, as we got onto the field, for some bizarre reason I walked up to Al and told him that he could have the Pavilion End while I would open from the Nursery End of the ground. I had never really enjoyed bowling from that end. On this occasion, I thought I would give it a go.

Al bowled well, but probably no better than he would have done from the other end of the ground. I, however, did not. Every over, I would drag one down and get cut. I knew that there was life in the pitch and plenty of movement if the ball was delivered in the right areas – I just didn't manage to do it. With Paul Prichard and Nasser Hussain both making scores, Essex got to 268 for 7 from their 50 overs. Mullally had figures of 3 for 36 from 10 and me 1 for 59 from 9. It was far more than they should have got, and I held myself responsible for that.

It then rained and we batted on the following morning after the pitch had been under the covers overnight. We were dismissed for just 76. It was an absolute disaster, and it was blatantly obvious that I had got things wrong throughout, including getting a 14-ball duck. I was out with us on 36 for 7.

I still go back to that game in my head from time to time and wonder why, for the only time during that season, I succumbed to Al and gave him the end he wanted. I still can't come up with a reason. It was the worst one-day performance of the year from my team, and I have been happy to put it behind me.

Overall, however, I must have impressed the bosses enough as captain because, in spite of being stood down during the latter part of the season for my tardiness, I was asked to be the club skipper for the following season of 1999. I turned the offer down, deciding instead to get on with simply playing my cricket. It wasn't a difficult decision at the time, but in hindsight I would have made a different choice. In truth, I was still upset and disappointed at the way I had been treated, even though I had put myself in that position.

With my decision to leave the captaincy behind, Vinny Wells was given the job in my stead. He was a good guy and I was 100 per cent behind him. He asked me if I wouldn't mind carrying on doing the team talks, and I agreed. I enjoyed trying to focus people's minds just before they went into battle. It was an important part of the game and I took plenty of pride in doing that job. Clearly, the kind of thing I was saying was having the desired effect.

That championship summer was dominated by Surrey who were at the start of their great run. Mullally had left for Hampshire, which was a big blow for Leicestershire. He never went for many runs in any competition and on his day he could make the ball talk. With Al and myself often taking early wickets, it made life easier for the second-string attack, which now included the very exciting prospect of Jimmy Ormond. He was medium-fast and could move the ball both ways through the air. He was also, rightly, a very confident man. But with Mullally gone, our overall attack could never gain the same control as we had before and our one-day cricket, in particular suffered. In the previous summer, we were always on the front foot, dictating games, but that was no longer the case. Although we ended up in third place in the championship, we all knew that we had lost some of our strength.

The World Cup rolled around again in 1999, the prestigious competition this time taking place in England. I had last played for my country in a couple of One Day Internationals against South Africa at the start of the previous summer, when my old surrey team mate Adam Hollioake had been made skipper of England. I then spent part of the winter of 1998/99 training and playing club cricket in Melbourne. While I was there, England were in town, so I went to see them play and bumped into Alec Stewart and the coach, David Lloyd. Both wanted to know about my fitness. 'I'm good,' I told them. 'You know me, training hard.' They told me that they wanted me to be in the team for the World Cup. I was as excited as a 5-year-old on Christmas Day. I had missed the 1996 tournament and was desperate to play in the tournament again, especially as it was on home soil. I was fit and working hard Down Under.

Back home, the 1999 season started well for me. I scored a hundred and took wickets in the first match of the summer against Essex. I then struck a second hundred before the end of April against Lancashire. Everything was going well. Then there was a strange exchange between Roger Goadby, CEO of Leicestershire, my manager at the time, Gareth James and allegedly the chairman of selectors, David Graveney. A message was relayed to me saying that I was going to be in the World Cup squad; this came from Roger, who had been speaking to David Graveney. However, when the squad was announced, my name was missing. SKY TV reporter Charles Colville was interviewing Graveney, and asked about how long it had taken to come up with the names for the squad. Graveney said that most of the players had picked themselves and the decision-making process had been a very easy one. One name, however, was discussed for three hours before being left out.

'Who was that?' Charles asked. 'Chris Lewis' was the answer.

My heart just sank. I put my head in my hands before half-looking at the television. I didn't really need to concentrate on what was being said. I knew I hadn't made the team. Gareth, my manager, was really pissed. He wanted to know why the selectors would tell me I was in the World Cup and then not pick me. We found out that there was a problem with me amongst members of the selection committee, that one of them did not want me in the squad. The captain, Alec Stewart, wanted me in the team; I knew that the manager, David Lloyd, wanted me in the team; and the chairman of selectors wanted me in the team. But I wasn't included – wow! The reason behind my non-selection, as I was soon to find out, was one of the selectors said that if I was picked he would resign. Funnily enough, I bumped into that selector a few weeks later. He came over, patted me on the back and told me, 'Unlucky, keep going.'

I knew it was all over. I just couldn't see a way back from here. If the three most important people surrounding the team wanted me to play and I still couldn't get in, then there wasn't much hope. Talk about the last-chance saloon, this was the no-chance saloon: no chance of playing for England ever again. I remember coming to that obvious realisation and, in that instant, some desire, some will, was lost: I didn't have as much to play for.

Before the World Cup got underway, I bumped into the England squad; I was playing a one-day game for Leicestershire in Canterbury where the squad were preparing for the tournament. I went in at number 5 with us in trouble on 14 for 3, and I made an unbeaten 116 and shared in a 220-run stand with Paul Nixon. We lost the game, but it was still satisfying for me to have got a hundred that day. I met up with some of the England boys after the match and I had a good time with them, with more jokes about not being good enough. I left them knowing that my cricket life was now all about playing for Leicestershire.

The rest of the summer did not go well. There was no lack of effort; I still wanted to do my job to the best of my ability. Things just weren't working out: something was lost, with neither the wickets nor runs coming as I wanted. I had always been a batsman who enjoyed the second half of the summer more than the first – flat wickets – but not this time. I saw some of the World Cup on the TV and England had a disastrous campaign, being knocked out before the knockout stages. I didn't gloat. A lot of the players involved were friends of mine, and who else would I have wanted to win except them?

9

SPOT-FIXING AND
THE STITCH-UP

As I've already explained, my international career was now over. Controversy had surrounded my cricket career for as long as I could remember, but I now simply aimed to put it all behind me and move on with my career at Leicestershire. But in the latter part of the summer things were to get a lot worse. The next moment of controversy in my career was to ultimately bring an end to my life as a professional sportsman.

During the summer of 1999, I was in Leicester and I had a call from my mum in London. She was in a local shop run by a Mr Patel, I had known him since I was a young boy. I often went in to his shop when I was at home in Harlesden. My mum would call from time to time saying that she had someone who wanted to talk to me; it was, quite honestly, a pain in the neck. But here was Mr Patel on the phone talking to me as if we were old friends. He explained that he had some business friends coming over from India who were interested in talking to me about some sort of business deal. Over the years, I had had many people propose business deals, and in the vast majority of cases they had nothing really to offer. Sometimes the people just wanted to meet me, or they might ask me to endorse their product with the chance of a payment somewhere down the line – payments which, in most cases, never materialised. I told him that I was too busy playing cricket and I was nowhere near London. I tried to be polite but I wanted to get Mr Patel off the phone as quickly as possible. Yes, Mr Patel, I do remember you, but I'm very busy playing cricket, and have no idea when I'll be back in London. So, I said goodbye to my mum with a deep breath and hoped that that was the end of it. The thought of going to the capital on a wild goose chase did not appeal.

A short time later, with some time off, I was heading to London to go out for dinner with some friends. Mr Patel called again while I was in the car. It was a coincidence. 'Chris,' he said, 'are you in London?' With a frown on my face, I had to admit I was on my way to London. 'Can you meet some business friends, they are here from India and would really like to talk to you. Can you meet them this evening?'

Before I headed out for dinner, I would be going to Harlesden to see the family. Mr Patel's shop was close by, so I decided to go and see him, to get rid of the aggravation more than anything. Mr Patel was at the front of the shop when I arrived. He welcomed me and asked me to accompany him upstairs to his family quarters. I sat down as he offered me a drink. I declined, as I just wanted to hear him out and then get on my way. He told me that his business colleagues would be arriving soon. About ten minutes later, three Indian gentlemen walked in, one of them very well dressed and very well groomed. He was wearing a tailored suit and was obviously the man in charge. We chatted about cricket and he appeared to be very knowledgeable about the game. It was a pleasant chat.

But, as the conversation wore on, it became quite clear what these guys were here for. They wanted to fix cricket matches. I immediately became uncomfortable and I wanted to extricate myself from this situation. I just wasn't interested at all. With my perceived reputation and all that had gone on in my career before, this was the wrong place, wrong time and the wrong conversation: my spidey sense was going off.

I looked at my watch, making it obvious that I wanted to leave, but the man went on to explain that they had £250,000 on offer. They would give me this total sum and I would try to pay four or five England players to underperform or do certain things within a game at certain times. He carried on, explaining that if somebody would underperform for £5,000 or £10,000 then what was left in the kitty would be mine. I quickly explained that I was not in the England team and was unlikely to be. However, this did not put him off at all, and he said that he wanted me to organise sorting out the players for him.

He was hell-bent on convincing me, and this is when he spoke about other players and how he had had dinner with them. He named them, and he pointed at specific matches and specific people within the world game, not just England players, explaining that what he was asking me to do was common practice among some high-profile cricketers – that was, according to him.

At this point, I could hardly contain myself. I told him that I would have to have time to digest what he had just told me, and that I had a prior engagement, so needed to leave.

Like most in the game, I had heard about match-fixing, that there were people walking around hotels with money in briefcases. Players used to discuss these things. Mostly, though, these were all rumours. I left that meeting at Mr Patel's shop, went outside and got into my car. This didn't feel good. Before I even started the engine, I called a good friend who was also my solicitor at the time. I told him what had just happened. The reason for that was to document the meeting. I had nothing to hide. The next call was to my manager, Gareth. I went back to my aunt's and cancelled my evening. Instead of the dinner with friends, I spent the time on the phone talking to Gareth. We discussed what we would do. My position was simple. I didn't want to be involved and just wanted to get on with playing cricket, get on with life. Here's why: I understood that, with my reputation, any involvement with match-fixing would be the death of my career. But, more importantly, I had never even thought about fixing a cricket match. Why would I when I always played to win, even if I was only taking on my little brothers in the garden? So, the notion of ever underperforming had never occurred to me. Why would I want to do that?

By the end of the evening, Gareth and I had decided that the best course of action was to report it to the ECB (England & Wales Cricket Board) and let them deal with it. So, first thing the following morning, I phoned Lord's to set up a meeting and to tell them what had happened. Before too long, I arrived at Lord's and met the Major for the first time. He was the press liaison officer to the England team. He suggested that we should go outside, and we sat overlooking the Nursery Ground. I recounted, step-by-step, all that was said at the meeting.

I left nothing out – nothing. I informed him of all that was said in the meeting and told him that there were three England players mentioned. I was asked if I believed what I had been told. I said no and that I was just recounting exactly what was said; there were no accusations from me at all. I didn't know the businessman from Adam, he had done most of the talking and within that he had mentioned players in world cricket who *he said* had been involved – again, not just England players.

I left that meeting at Lord's happy with what I had done. It was now over to the ECB to deal with the information I had given them. That included the name of a north-west London hotel where the businessmen were staying. They were going to call me later. I told all of this to the Major, and he simply advised me to tell them, when they called again, that I was not interested, I did exactly that. I must admit, I thought that the cavalry would be called in – flashing blues, like in *The Bill*. In fact, they called me on a couple of other occasions to find out if I could offer them information about pitches, or even information about team selection. I reminded them again that I simply was not interested in their plan. Job done – or so I thought.

A few weeks later, now in August, I was back at Lord's playing for Leicestershire against Middlesex. While I was playing, a member of the ECB came to see me and said that, after all, we should report the incident to the police, because what had occurred was illegal. So, we went to the station in St John's Wood, where I made a formal statement. Soon afterwards I was contacted by the police, and this led to many interviews. At the first of them, I recapped my story to the police. They asked for the names of the England players, which I supplied, as I had already done so to the ECB. It was my understanding that the next stage was for the police to talk to the board, which they did, and a formal investigation begun.

I met with the police on many other occasions, recounting various parts of the story, while they told me where they were in their investigation into the businessmen. They told me that betting in sport was quite common and mentioned a Chelsea football match when the floodlights went out. I was being educated about such things by the police, who clearly knew a lot more about how match-fixing was done than I did.

I tried to get on with my life and playing cricket. But when I turned up for training at Grace Road one day, somebody caught my eye. It was a reporter from the *News of the World*. He tried to get a conversation going but I was short with him. He talked about me reporting match-fixing, I acted deaf and dumb. I had only spoken with the police and the ECB in any real detail, but the reporter seemed to have a lot of information. It almost appeared as if he had a copy of my original statement to the board.

I declined an interview, but the story broke nonetheless. It was a story of an Indian businessman, a dark, subcontinental figure, trying to infiltrate English cricket, and about the corner shop owner who was used as his go-between. All of a sudden, life seemed heavy again. This story was never meant to get to the press. That was the whole point of going to the ECB, to let them deal with it. Now here I was again, centre stage. What a bitch.

Back on the cricket circuit, there was curiosity about what had been said, but there was also an air of, 'Why is Chris Lewis always causing trouble?' My Leicestershire teammates wanted to know more of what was said in the meeting above Mr Patel's shop – but this was not the stuff for idle chatter; it never was and never will be.

Physically I felt fine, but something had changed. From averaging close to 50 with the bat, I got a pair at Middlesex, and that average started to fall off a cliff. I played only seven more first-class games after that match at Lord's, averaging 10 with the bat and more than 40 with the ball. Although I felt fine, clearly I wasn't. The 1999 season ended in a murmur in a rain-affected game with Durham. Maybe, at last, there was going to be little stress relief, just get away from cricket, breathe a little bit while still training for the following summer. The new summer arrived, and at the time I could hardly have imagined that I would only have a handful of first-class matches left to play, and that the summer of 2000 would be my last as a professional cricketer.

Just before that summer began, there was a request through my manager for an interview for the *News of the World*. 'What about?' I enquired. There was a journalist who wanted to speak to me, to give my side of the story to the article that the same newspaper had published towards the end of the previous season: match-fixing. This seemed a little odd, as they already had the story. I had not spoken to the paper previously and so that article was gleaned from other sources and it seemed accurate enough, so why did they want to hear my side? But they were offering £13,000 to sit down with a journalist to tell the story. I agreed and told them the same story that I had told many times before, to the police and to the ECB. I was paid and carried on preparing for the new season ahead. I felt blindsided by what appeared in the newspaper. They wrote a piece about three England players being involved in match-fixing, and the general consensus was that I was accusing England players of taking money to underperform in matches. Let's stop for a minute. Let's be clear. I have never accused anyone of match-fixing, I knew the players that were mentioned during that meeting, I had played with them, they were great performers. The thought that they could be involved in any kind of match-fixing had never occurred to me, nor did

I believe it. Of course, the press wanted to know more and they began asking questions of the ECB: 'What do you know of Chris Lewis reporting match-fixing and the involvement of England players?' The governing body used a deaf-and-dumb attitude and claimed that they had no idea about any England players being mentioned as regards to match-fixing. They added that anyone interested should ask Chris Lewis about it; excuse me, did they just throw me under a bus?

This was the start of the dark times. My career had been filled with controversies: being late for matches, wearing the wrong clothes, shaving my head, and so on. They might have made headlines, but all this paled into insignificance: out of all the things I've been labelled through my career, this is the one that I can't stand. The general feeling was that I had maliciously made up stories about England players being involved in match-fixing for some financial gain. I didn't know what to say. I am not that way inclined – that was why I was never the one in committee rooms telling tales. This was the procedure the ECB had recommended themselves, the very thing they instructed us to do if approached, and yet now they had dropped me right in the shit.

In April 2000, I was called up to a disciplinary committee run by Gerard Elias QC. I went with my solicitor and I recounted, yet again, word for word, my encounter with the businessmen and with the Major. I could tell that he believed me. Why wouldn't he? It was the truth, detailed in multicolour.

I left the committee confident that things would now become easier. Instead, it was reported that I had given new information that the ECB would now look into. What new information? That suggested that at the first meeting I hadn't told them everything that I knew, and that was certainly not the case.

My manager, Gareth, was straight on the phone to them and some heated exchanges took place. Gareth did not mince his words. I was now beside myself with anger. All the other things I had done had been on my own head. I had made my own bed and had dealt with the criticism. But this? No, no, no!

Many things had happened up to this point of my life. I had been called 'the prat without a hat'. I'd been accused of not trying for England. I'd turned up late for Test matches. My commitment, and perhaps even my sanity, had been brought into question. But this, being accused of making up stories to get colleagues in serious trouble, was taking things too far. The ECB knew that I had told them all of this a year ago, as did the police. In fact, a policeman called me to apologise. They knew the truth, of course. If I had made all of this up, where was the charge for wasting police time? There were records of phone calls, hotel receipts and so on. The evidence was there. All you needed to do was look for it. But, I would have to scream and shout as long as it would take to get my side of the story in the open. Unfortunately, my voice didn't seem to be loud enough. These were the hardest of times. My dreams, my world, my life had imploded. My performances on the cricket field suffered and became almost non-existent. Being booed by supporters at the grounds and receiving letters calling me Judas were easily the worst moments of my life. Wanting to play cricket was the last thing on my mind.

My concern was simply how to deal with the situation I had found myself in and how to resolve it.

In the end, nothing was resolved. The ECB decided to take no action against me because they knew that I had done nothing wrong. I had a meeting with Lord McLaurin, chairman of the ECB at the time, where he talked about 'putting everything to bed'. McLaurin released a statement that said I should be allowed to continue my career and that I had shown guts in coming forward. But I had already been dropped in the shit. I was still majorly pissed off. I hadn't done anything to be ashamed of but I had been savaged in the media. They were having a field day at my expense.

These were the times that I stayed at home, not wanting to go out, in fact being ashamed of going out because of what people must have thought of me. How could my dream have come to this? The whole stigma towards me still stands to this day. I did the right thing, to the letter, but as far as my cricket career was concerned, it very much became the wrong thing. I gave the ECB the ball and they absolutely fucked it up. They had information, backed up by Stephen Fleming, who reported the same Indian businessman to the International Cricket Council (ICC), within forty-eight hours of me doing the same with the ECB. Yet I was still thrown to the wolves. I had contempt for that – I still do.

Some years later, in 2004, Fleming released his book *Balance of Power*, in which he recounted how he was told by a fixer in 1999 about the wide-reaching Asian sports gambling syndicates which held sway over such things as England football and international tennis. He also said that he was offered half a million by an Indian businessman to join a match-fixing syndicate in 1999 (yes– that's the same syndicate that approached me). At the time, a Kiwi journalist called me and asked me what it was like to be vindicated following the release of *Balance of Power*. I told him that I didn't feel anything. I always knew that I had told the truth from the beginning, I declined his offer of an interview.

With hindsight, I can see why the ECB wanted to keep things out of the public domain, but it doesn't excuse the way I was treated. There is nothing about those times I remember with any fondness.

If you think that would be the end of it, there was yet more to put on top. Throughout my career, people had wanted to get me out on the cricket pitch, even when I was not fully fit to play. But now, although I was fully fit, Leicestershire didn't select me for their games. The first thing I thought about was a clause in my contract which stated that if I didn't play a percentage of the matches then my contract could be terminated.

I went to see the team physio to ask him one simple question – am I fit to play? 'Yes' was the answer. I called an old friend who was now with the Professional Cricketers' Association (PCA), the players' union. I told him what was going on – I was not being selected, and I told him about the clause in my contract. I told him that Leicestershire were going to try and sack me at the end of the year, even though I had three years left on my contract and more than a hope of getting a benefit, which was agreed before I signed that six-year contract.

I was correct. At the end of the season of 2000 in which I played only five first-class games, I had a meeting with the club's chief executive, who told me of their intentions. I told them that I had seen them coming and that I didn't want to be at Grace Road any longer, I've had enough, I just wanted to leave, no thoughts in my head about what I would do next, how I would pay the bills. I keep saying that I was angry but that really doesn't describe how I felt at this time. The truth of the matter was that I was done. I didn't want to play cricket any more, for Leicestershire or indeed anyone, so I walked away. But I walked away as a different person: an angrier person, less patient, quicker to agitate, less smiley.

10

THE WILDERNESS YEARS

After leaving Leicestershire, life became different, very quickly. I had signed a long-term contact with the county with more than a hope of a benefit at the end of it: in fact, that had been agreed. Now, three years into that contract all was at an end. Of course, I had hoped that after my contract had ended and I had received a benefit that I would be in a place to be able to start life after a career as a professional sportsman.

But here I was, practically penniless, with few options, not having trained to do something else. It could have been all right, if it hadn't been for the injustice of what had just been done to me. I didn't know at this time that these feelings would stay with me for a long time. Of course, I had been angry in the past, but that anger had very rarely stuck. I simply didn't know at that time that this anger would be part of my life going forward and would cloud how I saw the world, my experience of it and perhaps even my ability to make the right or the best decisions.

What I didn't understand at the time was that this was playing the victim. Not consciously, because if anyone has ever asked me if I have been victimised I have responded with a firm no. I guess I just retreated into myself. I was easily annoyed. I became less tolerant and spoke with a raised voice. All of this was evident to my family, but at the time I thought it was a reasonable place to be, bearing in mind how I had perceived what had just happened to me.

There were things I now needed to do. I needed to find a new place to live for starters, and, of course, I would need work. But what would I do? I've never had a problem with cricket, as in the game itself, and even though I didn't want to be outside on a cricket field at this moment, the sport did give me a little hope. I could play cricket at the weekend, earn a wage, and not have to deal with any of the things that I had been dealing with before. Just play and then leave, don't get too involved.

Once I decided I was going to play club cricket, doors quickly opened up. One of the people who spoke to me was a man named Tyrone Brown who was coach, manager, nursemaid, organiser and overall supremo at a team called West Indian Cavaliers, based in Nottingham, where I was now living. Two old colleagues of mine also played for them: Greg Mike, formerly of Nottinghamshire, and Andrew Haye, formerly of Leicestershire. The team, as the name suggested, was made up of West Indians. After my recent experiences and – let's just say here – misunderstandings, West Indian Cavaliers seemed to be the ideal place for me. I would be around people who looked like me and talked like me, so perhaps they would be more understanding.

I became captain and played for the Cavaliers for two years. However, it didn't work out and soon enough I was on my way. You see, one of the things I was trying to get away from was what seemed like a constant sniping and people talking behind others' backs at the professional clubs I had been at previously. But here at the Cavaliers, the sniping and talking behind teammates' backs and generally trying to throw a spanner into everybody else's lives was practised at an almost professional level.

As well as playing for the Cavaliers, the club also tried a pilot scheme where I would coach young inner-city children with the aim of getting them off the street, giving them somewhere to go and something to do, and hopefully inspire them and change their lives. However, this all came to an end after two years. I was not going to deal with all the sniping again. Why can't people just get on with their jobs? What's all this behind the scenes stuff? It did my head in. I needed a quieter space.

What followed was a winter of unemployment, sitting at home on the couch with my thoughts; not good ones. It was a time where I was only processing the things that had gone wrong in my life. Thankfully, the next summer a friend suggested that I should come and play cricket at his club, Clifton in the Derbyshire Dales, just to get out a bit. I was apprehensive to start with; going into a new crowd of people, my mind would simply ask, 'Why would you want to do that?' But I did need to get out of my house. I felt better when I was outside, and running around a cricket field was still what I did best.

I spent a couple of years at Clifton CC where I met Ant Botha – who would later go on to play for Derbyshire and Warwickshire – and the club captain, Simon Moore who was a good club opening bowler, with fire in his belly. For the very first time in Clifton's history, we won the Derbyshire Premier League. Simon and the other guys at Clifton made life very simple for me. They were grateful for my efforts on the field and allowed me to be the person I was off it. It was a nice feeling for a while to wake up on a Saturday and look forward to playing cricket. It had been five years now since I had been a professional cricketer, and I couldn't say that I was earning a living but I did earn enough to eat – well, most of the time. So, here again, time was being spent without being particularly fruitful.

Then I was on the move again, heading back to the capital to play cricket at Slough and to open up my own cricket academy. I liked being back in London. I felt more at ease, fitted in more. I played at Slough for one year while coaching at the academy, which was also based in Slough. So, plans were set. Play and coach during the summer and focus on the academy in the winter. The real highlight was taking a group of 11–18-year-olds on a trip to Holland for a week and playing against a Dutch representative side. It was great seeing the excitement on the kids' faces; they had a ball. I guess they never imagined that they would go on an overseas tour as cricketers. They won games and I was sure that this was the way things were going to go from now.

But, while playing at Slough, I also turned out for the Professional Cricketers Association (PCA) and during one of these matches, against Essex in a Twenty20 game, for a few overs at least, it seemed as if half of Chris had come back with the ball. I think it was Martin Bicknell, a former Surrey colleague of mine, who thought I may be able to do a job. Over a period of months things developed until, one day, Surrey's captain, Mark Butcher, was on the phone. 'Flipping hell', I thought to myself, 'I can't believe this.' The chance to play Twenty20? That might just work. I would only have to bowl four overs. Surely, I could run around for four overs?

Later, Mark's dad, Alan, the coach of Surrey at the time, called me and a deal was agreed. I would play for Surrey in the Twenty20 competition but my contract, if you could call it that, would be a pay as you play deal. What the figure would be, I didn't know. I didn't care. It just seemed to be a good opportunity.

It was late in 2007 and I knew I needed to practise. As it was winter in the UK, I organised to go to Newcastle, just outside of Sydney, Australia. I would do what I was consistent at – training – in the hope of being ready for the 2008 Twenty20 campaign. I put together what money I could find and headed off to Australia. I would be there for three months. Of course, Australia is always great, but, alas, my body wasn't. It was like knowing your car has five gears but it can only find third. And there was the pain after the exertion – groin, hips, legs, calves, everything would light up. It would take a while to be able to bowl again. Nevertheless, I trained as hard as I could. After two months in the sun it was time to come back to London to be part of pre-season at the Oval: as much practice as possible. This was upping the workload.

The season started and I was in Staffordshire, playing club cricket, getting ready for the summer: overs under my belt. I bowled 26 overs on a cold and breezy afternoon. Again, that was training, just getting my body used to bowling again. But when I came off the field, there was a call from Alan Butcher back at the Oval. The gist of the conversation was that Surrey were short of players and they wanted me to play in the 50-over competition against Middlesex the very next day. I must admit that I remember thinking, 'wrong timing'. I had just bowled all afternoon and I knew my body would react to that. Of course, I was not going to say no to Surrey's offer, even though my agreement was just to play Twenty20. My hope was that whenever I came on to bowl the batsmen would take a few overs to have a look at me before realising that I was now just a pie chucker. However, the game had already moved on and I ended up with figures of 0 for 51 from 6 overs, Middlesex getting 315 for 6, a hundred for Andrew Strauss.

With the bat, I managed 33 runs, patchy to start with, but then I got one away off Shaun Udal and for a while it felt like old times. We were bowled out and lost the game easily. I had been caught on the long-off boundary by Eoin Morgan. There was still work to do to try to get up to speed before the Twenty20 started, more club cricket, more training.

Before too long, the Twenty20 competition had begun and the first game was at the Oval against Essex. I liked the buzz of coming into the ground with the spectators already there, the noise, the anticipation. We were starting the game in the early evening; this was different. I was going to enjoy this.

I was brought on first change by acting skipper, Mark Ramprakash, and my first ball was going to be to the Essex opener, Mark Pettini. I ran in, bowled length just outside off stump. What the fuck? The ball disappeared over mid-wicket for 6. I must admit, that over felt like there were nine or ten balls in it. It went on forever. In the end, I delivered two overs, going for 29 runs, not the best. But, there was still a large part of the game to go. I wandered into the outfield, and at least there I would be able to do some running. I remember diving at mid-on to stop a ball, landing on my side. It felt like I weighed a ton. I remember thinking, what an odd sensation it was, to hit the ground so heavily. I guess in the past I must have always anticipated the ground. I didn't this time, and I fell heavily on my hip. I do recall getting up and it was hurting but I had experienced all this before, many times. My body was warm, and I could still run around but I was in pain.

After the match had finished, which incidentally we were well beaten in again, the stiffness began, I could hardly get up to leave the dressing room. Maybe this would change with a good soak in the bath, a good night's rest, I've felt worse and played the day after.

A few weeks later, and there was no change. I could hardly put any pressure on my right leg and when I did, that leg would just give way; I still could hardly walk. The comeback was already over before it had really begun. What now? Somehow, I managed to turn out for Ilford CC for the rest of the summer – I simply needed the money – but this only made my leg worse.

The cricket season was now over and all that lay ahead seemed to be a winter of doing nothing and then another summer, but a summer without the ability to earn a wage on the cricket field. The summer of 2008 had not worked out and I had not earned even a fraction of the money I had hoped for. In fact, I was out of pocket. But, what was I going to do? I just felt like I needed space to think but I didn't have time to do that; I needed to do something now.

Looking back, I can recall the moment that it all changed. In my life, I have heard all sorts of conversations, been in all sorts of places, but most of them never concerned me; you see, I knew where I was headed. But now I found myself listening to all sorts: I was needier. Of course, I had received speeding fines and parking tickets in the past, but I had never done anything criminal. Now here I was, curious and even asking questions: 'really, I didn't know that, how much?' That quickly. None of this had ever interested me before. I didn't want to be a criminal. I remember my thought at the time: just once, maybe, to make a bit of money and give myself a little bit of breathing space to help me decide where to go next. If I did it quick enough, nobody would know. This was the time that the right side of my brain, if it had been working, would have been screaming, 'What the fuck are you thinking? Don't be so stupid, you think things are bad now, what if you get caught? Are you brain-dead?' I am ashamed to say that never happened. I was locked in; my mind only seemed to be working one way. All I could think of was the idea of having no money and not being able to see a way out. The future looked bleak. In what seems like no time at all, a hasty plan was arranged: I would go to St Lucia to import cocaine to the UK. My cut would be £50,000, this would give me the breathing space I needed. So I headed to the Caribbean island of St Lucia, with my co-defendant in this case – but I will leave him to tell his own story.

As for mine, people may suggest that I could have gone down to the dole office, could have got a job, and a hundred other things I could have done. And all of that would be true. But, I can tell you, I had got myself into such a fearful state that those thoughts never even occurred to me. Sitting here now with hindsight, all those things seem so obvious and elementary, but I was only talking to the devil at the time. Fear and panic can do that to you: shut off your real thinking process.

11

GUILTY

It's 20 May 2009. I have just been found guilty of drug smuggling. The judge wraps up the court proceedings and concludes with a lecture; the judge said I was motivated by greed, and as a previously successful sportsman I was a role model and an ambassador. I did not hear it. I was in a different world.

The only thing that matters to me now is how long I will be imprisoned. The words 'thirteen years' ring out around the court and drown out all other sound. For five months I have been dreading this moment and now here it is, my worst fears confirmed. The bleak future is laid bare, right before me. All those sleepless nights have been leading up to this, but I am still unprepared for the shock of those words. I don't know how to feel. 'Wow!' is all I can think. A long sentence was always possible, but the very thought of that sentence stretching out before me sends me dizzy. Think about it … thirteen years. I don't think I've ever planned beyond the next cricket season.

You see, I have never been a forward planner – something, if you have read this far, you will not be surprised to hear. The furthest I've ever had to look ahead is the cricket fixture list at the beginning of the season. I knew I would be at Worcester on a particular day or Nottingham on another, but apart from that I've tended to let life just happen. All of a sudden, I am trying to look thirteen years ahead. How can I possibly manage that? I do some sums in my mind – 156 months, 676 weeks, 4,750 days, give or take. Don't even think about minutes and seconds, counting them down as you wish your life away. How can I put a plan together over such a huge length of time? Although I don't know how I am possibly going to cope, my mind is already accepting that I will be in prison for a long time and that my release date is a distant point way beyond the horizon. Somehow, I thought that the trial would be the end of things, but of course it is really just the beginning of a long journey, and despite all the negative thoughts and all the stresses of the case, I am here and alive.

The officer takes me down to the cells beneath the courthouse, and there is a sense of relief that the court case is over and I won't have to face the glaring eyes of the public, I realise I won't be able to fully assess my situation and how I feel until I get back to my cell. At this moment, I am trying to hold myself together.

It takes some time for the bus to arrive to take me back to prison, and when I finally get there it is night and all the other prisoners are locked up, the place mostly silent. As I have missed dinner, some sandwiches have been left for me by the officers. Alone with my sandwiches I sit on the bed, and for the first time I actually look around the cell and take in all the detail I had missed before while on remand. I have no idea why I do this, or why I hadn't properly looked before. Perhaps it was a way of denying reality, but there is no point in doing that now. I will be here for a long time, a *very* long time.

As I sit here, I try and imagine what six and half years in jail means – because that is the least amount of time I will serve with good behaviour. Then I begin to dwell on all the things I am going to miss. For a moment, I tell myself to 'pull my socks up', but then decide that perhaps now would be a good time to let it all out: some of the emotion I have been holding inside ever since the fear took over back at Gatwick Airport months before. I begin to cry, not for long, maybe fifteen minutes or so, before I get a grip on myself. In that time, everything I was keeping inside pours out into that tiny cell, all the pent-up fear, panic and frustration just floods out. An officer checks on me through the flap, something they do routinely, but in this case it's because I have just been sentenced and am more of a suicide risk.

My mind is racing, and somewhere in there is the ghost of a plan I had for dealing with this situation. It involved tying bed sheets together, wrapping them around my neck and jumping. But now I am here, I realise that that was no plan at all. In the end, I just stare at the pictures on the wall and realise that they are a window into a life that I don't have any more. They are the symbols of false hope, and so I take them down and store them in my bag. If this is my fate then I am not going to play games with myself and allow these tantalising glimpses of another life, there is no point in pretending that I have a life outside these walls: that is gone.

Something interesting happens over the next few days. The panic and fear subside and I am not afraid. Now the sentencing is over and my immediate future decided, I know that I can do this. It is going to be a long road and it is going to be a pain in the arse, and I am not being flippant in saying that; it is just that I have new clarity and certainty that I will make it. I don't want to serve years in prison – of course not – but I also realise that there is absolutely nothing I can do about it, so I just have to buckle down and get on with it. There is already a goal in the distance, a long way in the distance, but I can still see it. I begin my life as a Category B prisoner, due to the length of my sentence – more than ten years. But the hope is to become a Category C prisoner as soon as possible, and then Category D. There is a review every year.

Prison is a very alien environment and a lot of the airs and graces of normal life are absent. Some inmates are used to getting their own way and often don't care about what others want or feel, it is everyone for themselves in here. A show of strength is important and decisiveness a necessity, as dithering is considered a weakness. And I have noticed that the people around me in jail thrive on weakness. Whatever I say, it has to be forthright, and I have to show that I am not wounded or affected by anything they have to say to me. I am here because I committed a crime, not to be a source of interest or amusement for other prisoners. This is a place where you can be eaten up very quickly, and I am not prepared to feed the needs of others by chatting about cricket or famous sportsmen I have met, or the life I have led. I just want to serve my time, not regale them with stories and anecdotes.

I get on with most of the staff. If there are any issues, then it is with the prisoners. I don't cling on to the bars screaming;

I don't call the officers 'screws', like the stuff you have seen in films. I don't think it is necessary to fit in. Basically, when people don't like you in these environments, there are two things they say: either 'you're a snitch', or 'you're a paedophile'. I don't consider myself to be either. I am 6ft 3in and I am okay handling myself. Physical presence helps a lot in here. The people that many of these guys respect the most are simply the biggest, the ones who go to the gym and appear to be the strongest. I am not that, but nor am I the one going around smiling trying to please everyone. This seems to work fine. There are no serious issues, so for most of my sentence I don't feel threatened and I am not scared of any physical repercussions. .

They're funny, some of the rules you find in prison: 'You can't snitch, you mustn't snitch' and if you do people in here would look to do you harm. That was the way. Why not? Who came up with this code of conduct? Which bloke decided all this in the first place, the code you are all following? Have you bothered to check it out to see if it serves you? It only serves the people at the top – in this case, those who would go around beating others up and then are shocked if anyone reported them. That isn't the done thing. But what would they expect you do? They are beating some guy up and there is no one to help him, and then on top of that you are not allowed to snitch. This, I understand, is a prison tradition; it has been this way for a long time. It just sounds like heaven for a bully. I'm not interested in any of this. In life generally, I weigh things up and if I agree with them, I might play along, but not if that is purely based on the fact that it has 'always been that way'. If I don't agree, then I'll say that it's shit and be on my way.

There is a certain amount of interest in me, I guess that's fairly natural as there was a lot of press coverage. The other prisoners have seen you on TV, and then they're standing right next to you or in the cell next door to you. It's a talking point for some people. The general consensus is that I have fallen from grace – the classic tale. I suppose that makes the story interesting to certain kinds of people. Everybody in here is here for a reason and I am just another prisoner. As you would expect, the officers here treat me the same as all the other prisoners. There are some who are cricket fans, and I suppose they're not terribly impressed by what I have done. There is curiosity from a lot of people, officers and inmates alike.

I am asked if my life has been a party. Yes, it has, but only a medium-sized one rather than a great big enormous one with all the trimmings. But the problem with the parties I have lived through is that when I look at my bank account, there is nothing left. I don't divulge too much about my career. It's fine to be polite and say hello, but to spend my time answering questions about Brian Lara and Ian Botham – always Ian Botham – it does become a bit of a bore, so I set my stall out. Within a month of my sentencing I am heading north to a new prison; Dovegate, near Uttoxeter. I am automatically categorised as a Category B prisoner and Dovegate is one of the few options. The new prison regime is strict, with pretty much every move being monitored or escorted, even to and from the visiting room. It's not exactly like the old-fashioned chain gangs you saw in some movies, but there are similarities. There are extra gates, more guards and less freedom.

My stay at Dovegate lasts a year, and I devote much of my time there to reading. My choice of reading matter largely involves self-help books or those with a spiritual content, something I was into prior to my incarceration. It is important to stress that it is not my arrest and sentencing that has led me down this path, it was one I had already chosen. The only difference now is that I have significantly more time to devote to reading and also the realisation that this type of literature can improve my state of mind, which is the absolute key to surviving this ordeal. So I read more and more, and the message is clear: I must take responsibility for what I have done in the past, will do in the future and for my actions here and now. So much of what has happened to me was not consciously decided upon, it just sort of happened, and that is the pattern of behaviour I must change. What I read strikes a chord with me. It is about being in the present, about noticing and realising what I am doing, choosing and thinking about, and what I did that put me in places and situations I didn't want to be in. What is it about me that attracted so much negative publicity throughout my playing career? Have I deliberately courted controversy? If so, why? What thought processes led me into smuggling drugs and then prison?

It becomes clear that I have not been self-analytical enough, and so now I am examining even the safest of my choices and trying to hold them up to the light. I quickly realise that the negative thoughts I've had previously have no place in this new mindset taking root.

For a time, I am in a kind of mental no-man's-land. I'm not sure of what's going on in my head, but at least I have a tool for dealing with some of my negative emotions and thoughts, a way to find a bit of quiet. Despite being surrounded by negative cues, I am able to stay positive. If I start to stray down a negative road, I say to myself, 'Hang on, Chris, what are you doing? Why are you terrorising yourself?' Oddly, I find this quite amusing, and that raises my spirits and helps me to realise that I have a choice about whether I continue with the negative thinking or whether I make a change and move on to something more positive.

This jail is a curious place. I can't really talk to others about my sentence of thirteen years, you see. That's because it is such a small sentence compared to the prisoners I am now around; most of these guys are serving life sentences. Many have already been behind bars for eighteen years or more and they are still Category B, so they don't want to hear me going on about my comparatively short sentence. Curiously enough, I don't want to talk about it either: it terrifies me.

Over several months life has become routine, as you would expect. I eventually get a job in the gym and can get back into some sort of training regime. My job is being a gym orderly, which involves cleaning and tidying the gym, but I fit in a few games of table tennis when I can, after the real work is done. This is how I pass the days as they mount up and merge.

Time passes, and before I know it a year has gone by and I am being reassessed. (OK, the year didn't quite fly by as quickly as reading that sentence, but it does pass far faster than you could imagine.) My review is standard after the first year of incarceration. Its purpose is for the prison board to look at the risks I present and move me to Category C if they feel that the risk is low enough. What that means is a prison where not every door needs to be opened by an officer and where there is more freedom. I can walk to and from my healthcare appointments by myself; it may not sound much, but it's a step up the ladder.

Tiny steps are what the prison system is all about. Good news: my review is successful and I become a Category C prisoner. I am not sure how that was decided, but I haven't got myself into any trouble. So, I will be on the move again and hopefully heading closer to London, where most of the family and friends are. Getting to Dovegate to visit was hard work for them, taking all day.

I am taken to a prison called The Mount in Hemel Hempstead. This is where I do most of my sentence. I spend three years here, and it's day-to-day living. I do many jobs in that time. I am an 'insider', which means I meet and greet new inmates and teach them the ropes – the way the prison system works – and help them to bed in. But I spend most of my time in the workshops. I do courses on painting and decorating, bricklaying, cookery and psychology. In this way I keep myself busy, but I am also doing courses that I hope will be useful. That pretty much takes care of my time at The Mount: one mundane day after another. Life, at this stage, seems rather predictable.

One day, it's time for my D-Cat review again, as it is mandatory for the jail system to do that. So far at The Mount, I have always been denied because of the length of time I have left on my sentence: you can only go to D-Cat, if you have two years or fewer left on your sentence. For the first time in years, I'm excited. Becoming a D-Cat prisoner would mean an open prison. There I would get the opportunity to start rehabilitation, through working in the community and being able to go home to loved ones. I could begin making amends. That would mean the world to me: the opportunity for more freedom within the jail and finally the possibility of being let out for a day to go and visit the family. That would be amazing, just for them to see that I'm doing well and that I'm okay. *I* know that I'm doing alright, but it will be great to show them that. I try to imagine what it has been like for them for the last four and a half years. Seeing them again in the outside world would take a bit of that pressure off.

So, I wait. Finally – and it seems like an eternity, although it must only be a month after the review process began – one day I get back from work and on my bed is a folded piece of paper. I pause for an instant and then start walking slowly towards it. I pick it up, take a deep breath and open it slowly. My eyes scour the paper, trying to find the relevant information. Two simple words, I am looking out for – granted or denied.

I don't believe it: 'Denied'. The letters seem enormous on the page. I've been denied. But for what reason? I have tried to be the model prisoner, keeping my head down and trying to use the experience for exactly what it is intended – rehabilitation. I read the document more thoroughly and it says that I haven't finished all of the courses I needed to do on my sentence plan. A sentence plan involves courses, whether behavioural, drug/alcohol courses, or any others that the prison service believes you need as part of your rehabilitation. I had applied for a course – enhanced thinking skills – but there was such a backlog that I hadn't been able to get on it. Those who are close to release are more of a priority for these courses, and because I still have two years to go I was at the back of the queue and never seemed to move up the list.

I appeal, and that takes two weeks. In jail, whenever I set my mind on something and have to wait, time seems to go very slowly even though it's the same routine. So I wait, again. One day, I get back to my cell from work and there is that piece of paper on my bed again. This time, I don't pause. I just open it, working my way down, looking for those two words again. This time: 'D–Cat granted.' Wow.

For the last four and a half years this has been my focus. First I tried to survive a year, then two or three, setting little goals not too far away. Now after four and a half years, I am almost there, Category D. Why is that so important? After four and a half years of constantly being watched, four and a half years of no privacy, four and a half years of being ordered around, the thought of private moments with loved ones and friends, without having to look over my shoulders: priceless. Now that it has happened, I almost can't believe it.

I slouch on the bed, just savouring the moment. It feels good. Soon, I will be able to see my mum, my brothers and my aunt. It's the first time anything seems *soon* in a long time. Yes, I can use that word again. It's one that I haven't needed for a long time.

I think that I just don't care where the Category D prison is, even if it's Timbuktu. I just want a day out to see the family. Where they send me is unimportant. A month passes and then I'm told that I'm heading to Hollesley Bay prison in Ipswich. I've never been to Ipswich.

12

THE BEGINNING
OF THE END

I arrive at Hollesley Bay Category D prison in Ipswich. There is no wire or brick fence surrounding the jail, and there is a public road that runs right through the prison: buses and cars, with real people in them. It would take a while for me to get used to this. I struggle to get my head around it all. You see, I've always had an image of this jail in my mind – without the barbed wire fence, without the guards walking around constantly checking on you, making sure you're not up to something. I'm still in jail, but here at Hollesley Bay it just doesn't feel like it. It is messing with my head a bit. I have been through the system, and have been deemed trustworthy enough: I am not an immediate or significant risk to society.

So, here I am. What does this mean? It means that, in a couple of months, after I've done my lay down, checks and assessment, potentially I can go home for a few days. But for two months, it's back to what has become normal – setting that goal and work towards it. The time moves slowly; somehow this wait seems harder than all the time I've already done. Then the day comes and I am ready; I have passed all the assessments, all the checks, all that I needed to pass, to be deemed safe to the public, I can go home.

This is real excitement. I'm tingling, literally, I can feel that tingling all over my body, and when I think about the family and the relief I hope they get in seeing me out of jail, a stress I caused, I can hardly control myself. Life has moved on so quickly in four and a half years, all my brothers and sisters have had babies, four and a half years of not seeing my new nieces and nephews. How do I feel? Good.

It's interesting, getting ready for my first home visit in almost five years. For a moment fear tried to take hold again. It makes no sense. I am now worried about whether I'll know how to catch a train. Have things changed so much in five years that I wouldn't know how to catch a train? I worry whether I'll be able to cross the road. It has been a while since I had to think about crossing a road. For five years, I haven't had to care about what was coming, left or right. It's stupid, but it's funny what your mind can focus on when you get used to worrying, it will pick on anything. I hear my name being called over the tannoy, time to go to reception, to get on the bus which will drop us to Ipswich train station before getting the train in to London. When I say us, I mean all the prisoners who are going home for a couple of days. As soon as I get on the bus and it leaves the prison I feel different; there is no prison officer on the bus, a sense of freedom washes over me.

When I get to the station there's a little apprehension, but when I go to cross the road, I do look left and right instinctively – that's a relief. I'd have hated to have to learn that all over again. At the train station, I get my ticket with a voucher given to me by the jail and off I go.

Home. The emotions are racked up so high that is hard to compare to anything else. I am so happy. But am I? Now I'm out of jail, the excitement is not quite the same. Where the hell has that gone? I work out that excitement has been replaced by a sense of relief. I thought that today somehow would be a day of celebration, but now I'm just relieved that I'm over the worst and I can put a smile back on my mum and aunt's faces. That was so emotionally hard, looking into their faces and seeing the pain I caused by putting myself in this position.

It will be nice to be able to start interacting again with my nearest and dearest. Being in jail is almost like being a child. Everybody else has to do things for you, even the simplest tasks, and what can you do in return? Nothing. So, it is just so nice to be able to start interacting again on a more equal footing.

In the time I have been away, I've acquired new nieces and nephews. Fortunately, the young ones are all well drilled – 'Hello, Uncle Chris!' – how delicious is that? Not to knock any of the grown-ups, but you can't match walking in and really, for the first time, being able to interact properly with these kids. They've all been told about Uncle Chris and they jump on me like they do with all their other uncles. It is a real joy, a very special moment that brings a tear to my eye. They are so beautiful, and I can't believe I haven't been here to play my part – take them to the park or to shop, spoil them a lot – but this is a real joy.

With the other members of the family, it's a relief to look into their faces and see them smile, genuine smiles that I haven't seen in years. It's amazing. Time runs so slowly on the inside, while my four days at home go by so quickly. But at least it will only be twenty-eight days before I can come home again.

Back in jail, things are different now. There is less there for me. There never was much there in the first place, but I suppose I had to find a focus, a coping mechanism, a way of getting through. Now, though, I've had a taste of life outside again, life at home, and being back in jail seems so pointless. All I can think of is my next home visit, another month away. The twenty-eight days between home visits move at a snail's pace. Before, weeks and even months would pass by quickly. Now I am looking at the calendar every day. What is becoming clear is that there is a slightly different challenge in Category D. While I was in closed conditions, there was no hope of ever going home, no hope of a day out, so I never gave it much thought (or, if I did, it was maybe a distant thought for the future). It quickly becomes apparent that what I considered the worst part of my sentence, mentally, isn't over yet. Now, it is a case of having to manage myself and manage the outside world – which, for the last four and a half years, I have kept at bay. Yet I yearn to be outside again permanently.

I get a new job. I'm an insider again, which means that I meet new inmates coming to the jail. I explain to them how the jail works and help them in their first few days in their new environment. I do this for six months, which takes me to the end of the year. I am then able to start doing some community work, which for me involves working for a charity. I start my first day at Ipswich Housing Action Group (IHAG). I'm going to be a chef; that's good for me, I know my way around a kitchen. IHAG deals with people of all types who have fallen on hard times: the homeless, people with alcohol and drug issues, and those with financial problems – a whole host of people in need of help. We point them in the right direction for benefits or treatment, and we also provide food parcels and warm clothing, helping where we can. The people here give out advice, they do the work, the charity work. And it's understood that people who are hungry don't make good listeners, so I do the cooking and help as a handyman. I cook breakfast and lunch. I'm here five days a week. It's an unreal experience. I meet all types of people, all of whom have found themselves here, in need of help, for a whole host of reasons. A general judgement doesn't fit all. These are people with alcohol problems, drug problems and a lot of their family relationships and friendships have broken down. It's a last resort centre. In the midst of all of this, there are people who have just fallen on hard times. It's curious to see that, whatever state people arrive here in, they did have a life before – as oil rig workers, lawyers, all sorts of professions. Yet, they have all ended up here.

It is an emotional place to work. Some days things seem to run smoothly, but on other days, the ambulance is called two or three times. One of our clients may have taken an overdose. On more than one occasion, I arrive to find one of the clients has taken an overdose and is propped up against the door. Sometimes I'm unsure whether they are even still alive. We call the ambulance and hope for the best. On other days, I come to work to hear that Peter, John or Sarah had taken an overdose and died overnight. But, hang on, I think, it was only a matter of hours ago that I was serving them lunch. It is a challenging environment, but one I seem to thrive in.

The people who work at IHAG are the real heroes of this part of my story, dealing with everything that is thrown at them. They know how to handle the clients, as they are called. They are kind, caring, and seem to understand what is needed ultimately: self-empowerment. It's a real learning experience for me.

I spend a year working with IHAG. The people I meet there are so gracious. They all know my situation, they all know what I've done and they all know where I've come from. Yet, they treat me wonderfully. This is my first time back in the community and it's nice to feel like a human being again. It would have been so easy for them to be judgemental and to be an extension of the jail, but it was nice to be around normal people – people who are not prisoners or work for the prison system. I have interacted well with officers for the years I have been a prisoner, but they are always your bosses. Here, though, I am part of a team. Yes, I'm just cooking in the kitchen, but I am part of the team and can take courses that are available to the staff. I am encouraged to take part in it all.

Eventually, my time is up: there are six months left on my sentence. There's one more thing I need to do, I want to learn to be a plasterer. There is a course back in the jail that lasts for five months, so I leave IHAG – with some regret. After all, this means that I will be back in jail seven days a week, day and night. But plastering is the last thing to tick off my list. I've been wanting to do it for some time now, and this is my last chance. Leaving IHAG is emotional, if I am honest. I've enjoyed my time working here and the people I have been with are genuinely nice. We have lunch, kisses and hugs. We will meet again, I tell them. They all seem to be pleased about that. They are tremendous people doing tremendous work.

I start the plastering course. It's fun, it's hard work, it's me. I like it. By day seven, I'm getting the hang of it. I can't believe it – I've cracked it. In reality I haven't, but that's my thought. It goes on for another four months. Each day, getting better. I'm not a professional, but I can do it – plaster that is – and I'm happy with that.

I'm now down to two weeks left. Okay, even two weeks is going to be long. My mind has changed – it's outside now; it's not in jail anymore. My body is still inside, but not my mind. So, now I'm on a forklift-driving course – that will kill another week! I learn to drive a forklift, and now I've only got a week left. The prison must organise my paperwork and there are various boards or meetings I have to attend to get myself ready for that day, one I have had in my mind since the beginning of my sentence.

13

RELEASE

I've had this day in my mind for more than six years – since the day I was sentenced. I had quickly done the maths, 'Thirteen years, so you will have to serve six and a half years in jail, and then six and a half years on licence': 9 June 2015 was the earliest date my nightmare could possibly end, and now I am almost there. There are just four days to go. I'm looking out of the window from my cell, thinking that it's finally over, 'I've done it,' In that moment, a funny thing happens. I feel the stress lift off my shoulders. I knew that over the last six and a half years I had been stressed; I would look in my own eyes and see it instantly. But I never realised how stressed I really was, how much weight I was carrying around on my shoulders, until that moment, when I felt it all lift away. I think I might be standing upright for the first time in a very long time. It's not that there is nothing to worry about now, just that this chapter is coming to an end and it's just a question of walking out through the gates in four days' time; it's a new beginning. The next part starts once I'm out: the rebuilding.

There seem to be a lot of people who think that being released from jail, after years of incarceration – with all the challenges that now lie ahead, economically and mentally – could be scary. But I'm just excited to have the opportunity to try again. I have witnessed some prisoners who, having been in jail for a long time, when it was time for them to leave they didn't know how they would function in the world that they had left behind; some had to be literally pushed out of the prison doors. Me, I don't think about it that way – there are fears, of course. I am aware how many people view ex-prisoners, it is a tag that has a lot of stigma attached to it. It's hard to get work. For many, it's hard to adapt to the outside world, some simply can't cope with crowds and may still yearn for what became comfortable to them: prison life. But I simply let the excitement of being so close take over. There is so much to do. There isn't the comfort of going back into cricket and the life I once had. Those days have clearly gone. I will be starting from the bottom up, but somehow I see it all as an exciting challenge. Ah, there he is, the Chris I know: up for it. He's been missing for a while.

It's the morning of release, I'm going to be released in a couple of hours. I could cry with happiness, but I am around prisoners, so there's not too much crying done here. I get ready, I should be out hopefully by 9.30 a.m. My brother and a friend are there to pick me up. I say my goodbyes, but I can't wait to leave. We drive out of the prison. 'Wow, Chris, look what you went and did. You've done well to survive that, but it could have been very different,' I say to myself.

It feels a little weird to have my freedom again, I've got used to the rules of the establishment and it takes time to remember that I'm a free man – I forget all the time and have to remind myself. Sometimes, at night, I forget that I can walk around the whole house. I was always in my cell by early evening in jail. There are lots of habits to change.

The support I have had from many people over the years, both whilst in prison and now back in the community, has been humbling. On being convicted for a drug offence, everybody is entitled to whatever stance they choose to take. Everybody makes decisions at these moments. You, the reader, may have already have made up your mind about who I am and what I did before you started Chapter 2, or even before you started the book. Friends and family are just that; they will support you through thick and thin to the best of their ability, and mine have been fantastic. But, outside of them, who would want to know me now?

One of the groups of people that came forward just when they were needed was the PCA, through Jason Radcliffe, the assistant CEO of the players' union. Right from the beginning to the end he was there, visiting all the far-flung jails that I found myself in, asking me how I was doing and whether I needed anything. Jason has been a friend and a supportive and positive voice, right from the beginning, when it was hard for me to see the light, to this very day. The support that he and the PCA have given has been at a more practical level now that I'm a free man, but the backing throughout has been invaluable.

Some people couldn't come to visit, but they wrote letters instead or sent messages, and when they were received they all helped in some way, giving me strength or helping me to access the strength I have inside. Those letters and messages meant I was still worth something. They gave me the energy to carry on because somebody still cared. I suppose one of my fears was that I'd made such a big mistake that nobody cared. But those people showed me that that wasn't the case. I felt so grateful for every message. The thing about jail is it can turn you hard if you don't have any outside reference point; it's a coping mechanism. If you perceive that nobody loves you then you tend to try to behave as if love doesn't matter. Sometimes these letters just asked, 'How are you?' yet that could light up a whole week.

One perfect example is the Smith family – Robin, his wife Kathy and his brother Chris – who wrote to check on my welfare, lifting my spirits, sending pictures of the growing Smith family, all the way from Australia. Kathy never forgot a birthday. I want to take this opportunity to say a big, heartfelt thank you to them, and to everybody who wrote a letter, came to visit, or sent messages of encouragement. Even those who couldn't do that, but still thought of me. Where I was, these small things made a big difference and just made me clearer about what I had to do, or who I want to become.

Now, walking in the community I grew up in, this is reinforced. These are the people, the community, who could be offended most, but all I get is, 'it's nice to see you', 'it's good that you are back', 'we are pleased to see you' and 'we're glad it's over for you'; in this way they say to me, *you have done your time, move on*. It shows a level of care. I'm emotional about the people around me and all they have done for me during this period of my life. My reaction is, 'Wow, that's such a beautiful thing you did, supporting me when I had nothing in return to give you.'

I don't know if I would have been able to survive my ordeal without the help of family, friends and, in some cases, complete strangers. Thank you.

On the first day of my release, in a car and heading into London as a free man, at last, I look around and see a hundred normal, everyday people going about their normal lives. And now I am a part of them again. It brings a smile to my face. It's funny, as it feels so good to be sitting here as a free man, at this moment, not needing anything, just happy to be free and to able to take part in life. It's an unusual experience, but then there have been a lot of unusual experiences in the past decade. Back at home, my family and friends are there and I can sense the relief in the atmosphere. Not so much the relief for themselves but relief for me that this chapter is now behind me. Personally, I am also relieved – that the pain that I've caused to my family and friends is over and I can now start to repair.

Immediately, I do an interview for the PCA, my support group. I did something wrong, it was a big mistake, and I need to apologise, set the record straight and own up to what I've done. And – most importantly – say sorry to everyone: my friends my family, my community and the people at large. I'm nervous and apprehensive, but I need to do this before I can attempt to move on.

At some point during my time in jail, I thought about moving on, about life after I left its confines. What was clear was that I had made many mistakes. It was important to own up to them, because it was the right thing to do and because for myself I needed to get things off my chest. Hopefully in time I can use my experience to help others, so that they can avoid the errors I made. What seems to be glaringly obvious is that I have made many mistakes during my cricket career and in the years since, but most have been my learning experiences: my adventure, my life. The only thing I really regret is breaking the law. Everything else I did to myself; this I did to others.

So, I do an interview with the PCA and one soon afterwards for the BBC. They are both about facing up to the facts, 'yes, I did do it', but also letting people know that that's not who I am, or who I would choose to be, regardless of the situation, ever again. Being a free man again, there are still fears – different fears, but fears nonetheless: an obvious one, fear that from here on in I will only be remembered as a convicted drug smuggler. I don't want to be defined that way, but if you do the crime you must take your licks.

But right now, I can only see the positive, and that's where I need to focus.

14

THE WORLD OF NOW – 2016/2017

It's an interesting time being back on the outside. I'm seven years removed from things and the world has changed; it didn't seem to change that much in the years before my incarceration, but in a short space of time since being in jail even simple things seemed to have moved on a lot. The processes have changed. It's nice to have some good people around who can show me how this new world works. Phones, messaging and the Internet have moved on at a great pace. I am not even in the know about cricket.

Then there are passport and ID issues, As part of my sentencing I have a four-year travel ban, so my passport has been confiscated. My driving licence has been lost, so applying for a new driving licence has been problematic. I haven't got the right ID. It's funny having to prove that I am me. Of course

I'm me. But in my new world, if you don't have the right ID, then you're not you. Having no passport and no driving licence closes a lot of doors and, of course, makes the process of moving on a little harder and longer.

In November 2015. I start my first job since leaving jail. I did work for a year at a charity in Ipswich as part of my reintegration back into society, but this is different. I am working at a building contractors, Tomlinson's, in Nottinghamshire. It is a friend's business. I work only in the office, my criminal conviction meaning that I'm not allowed out on site.

Soon, it's the New Year. In March 2016, I start a tour, organised by the PCA, to all eighteen first-class cricket counties. I am excited at the prospect; it's been fifteen or more years since I have been to some of these grounds. I am also a little bit nervous. How will I be received? What will they think of what I've done? I get over this by telling myself that it doesn't matter; what matters is the message I give, whether or not I can articulate that mistakes made earlier in life can and do come back to haunt you.

The first date is at Edgbaston. I arrive early. I don't want to be late. It's a rookie camp with players on their first professional contract. What are they going to make of this? I start to tell them my story. I tell them that what happened to me was avoidable. If only I had used my time in cricket to plan for a future that was bound to come. Even if you are one of the fortunate ones that manage to forge a career in professional sport, it lasts a relatively short time. I tell them that I have sat in their position many times and did not take the advice on offer. I remember thinking at the time, 'What do I need a pension for?' And if I did, I could sort it out later. There were no thoughts then about planning ahead. I tell them all that this was a big mistake on my part and that the best time to start planning for the future is right now. Take advantage of the PCA and what they have to offer, educate yourself, pursue other passions when possible, get yourself ready now for a day that will inevitably come. I tell them how fortunate they are and to have the PCA; the organisation has improved so much over the years. Then it's over to the questions and answers. The questions are gentle; those that ask them don't seem to be sure whether to probe too far. What was it like being in jail? What are you doing now? Trickier questions are to come later as the tour continues across the country.

Everywhere I go, people smile and greet me warmly. I could not have hoped for a better reception, all things considered. But I certainly hope that the message I want to share gets through. That message is not just for cricketers but for all professional sportspeople — to plan for the future. It seems such a simple and obvious message, but you can get caught up with being young, thinking that you will make enough money that you don't have to plan, and before you know it something happens and it's too late. Work on your personal development, try new things alongside your sport and learn something you have always wanted to learn. A broadened horizon helps to give more options for the future. These are all the things I neglected to do, things that did not seem to be important at the time, and now here I am, trying to convince an audience of their importance. I am the poacher turned gamekeeper.

After the initial apprehension, I enjoy the tour very much. It was nice to be in this position, trying to make a difference. It was also important on a personal level to be able to stand in front of a cricket audience and tell my story. I had thought it might be a little embarrassing, and I wasn't sure what sort of reception I would receive, but I enjoyed it very much and my audience seemed interested. I hope they got something from it.

I've talked earlier in this book about falling out of love with cricket, I am pleased to say that's not the case anymore; I really want to play. It has been seven years since I last played. Just saying that sounds strange. I've played cricket all my life, it reminds me of being a little boy and where I came from, where my great adventure began. I've missed it.

So, it's back to where it all started. Wembley CC, north-west London. I also play a few games for Lashings, a team of mainly ex-pros. We go around the country playing exhibition matches. It is enjoyable to be in that environment again; it is what I know. Alas, the body isn't up to it yet. I guess it's back to the gym. But I will try again next year.

It's funny how life just feels that much better now. I am still very blessed, not just to be here to carry on my life but also for the life I had before. Moving forward, I would love to show what I've learned, share my experience so that others do not make the same mistakes that I did, whether that is to a cricket audience, a wider sports audience or to the audience I left behind in jail.

Some of my experiences were not pleasant, so if I can stop just one person repeating my mistakes, then it would be worth it.

15

SO, WHO IS THE REAL CHRIS LEWIS?

Hindsight is a great thing. But, of course, it only comes after the fact. Looking back over all that has happened during my career, one thing becomes blatantly obvious. Through all my woes and my worries, things going wrong and things falling apart, the one constant was me. Eventually, when things die down – in my case, being in jail and having time to think – it's amazing how everything becomes a lot clearer, including the part you have played in your own misfortune, and your unwillingness to take full responsibility for what's happened in your life, even preferring to blame the outside world for who you've become. Yes, many things have been done by others, but ultimately what became clear was that the person who had the biggest influence on how things turned out was, of course, me. I read something – I can't remember who the quote is by – but it really captures what I mean: what others do to me is their karma; my reaction to what they do is my karma. Once I understood that, I realised that, at the crucial moments in my life, I had failed miserably. It was the beginning of looking at my life in a different way; I was trying to look in the mirror a bit more.

I remember heading off to Leicester as a young boy, all excited about dreams yet to be fulfilled. But I hadn't done my homework. I was ill-prepared for the adventure. I had no idea about what went on and what was expected of me. In truth, I didn't really care; I just wanted to play cricket. I thought everything else would take care of itself. Of course, it wasn't that simple. Me not knowing about the traditions of the game off the field – going to the pub after matches, meeting up socially, or even sharing the same jokes – meant that a space was created in which I could be accused of being all sorts of things: being lazy or uncaring, even wanting to destroy cricket clubs. I've never wanted to destroy anything. I was just doing my own thing. I understand now that my quietness, lateness, unwillingness to go to pubs or spend more time with my colleagues after cricket was always going to be problematic. But at the time I just couldn't fathom why people were being so nosey. It certainly got my back up. Was this two cultures colliding or just different ways of doing things? I suppose they might be the same thing.

Sometimes, I look back and I cringe at the things that I believed in those days, the things I expected. Here I was, not long since arrived from South America, going into Middle England and expecting the people to be like I was. Of course I hadn't thought it through. I hadn't thought about it at all. How foolish. So, in some ways, this was always going to be a problematic time. There I was thinking, 'What a weird bunch of people. What bizarre behaviour.' And naturally they were thinking exactly the same. Two sides not understanding each other.

I grew tired of hearing how talented I was and that it all came naturally to me, that I didn't have to work at my game and how fortunate I was, a natural fielder. I used to think how convenient it was for people to think so. To me it seemed to say that I didn't work at my game and everybody else did. That's why they could call me lazy. Of course, if you think about it, it's obvious that I could only play international cricket by working hard. It's not that I was blessed with something that others don't have. I was told that I was a natural in the field. But look around the world and see how fielding standards have gone through the roof. Why's that? Because they work at it. But that wasn't part of the agenda. The agenda was to prove that I was lazy. To admit that I worked hard and that it was my hard work that got me there would be to give me too much. But that was my just deserts, because I had worked hard. I was in the gym while others were still asleep; I was practising late at night; I was running on the streets at 6 o'clock in the morning. Ask anybody who really knew me. Ask Devon – we would often laugh about it. Devon once said to me, 'If only they knew, Chris, that you went to the gym before you came to the cricket ground.' Don't get me wrong, I can see how my behaviour played in to the general perception of me. My lateness gives an impression that I did not care about my sport. As I write this, I can only smile at some of my, let's say, mishaps. Some of my coaches and colleagues must have been tearing their hair out; I hope they can smile about it now.

So my world, as I experienced it at that time, was an agitated one. I remember meeting a supporter at Luton Airport. He came up to me and told me that a funny thing had happened. He was listening to the radio and the commentators were talking about me – how lazy I was and that I needed to do more of this and more of that. He said that he thought, 'How can this be case?' He thought I was the best athlete in the side, the best fielder and that I could hold my end up with bat and ball. Yet I was the one being called lazy. He said that he called the radio station to put his point of view across, but that when they found out what questions he wanted to ask he was cut off. Now, all of these things bring a smile to my face. They don't cut as deep, nor feel as personal. In fact, they seem to add a little more flavour to the experiences.

Sitting here, I cannot believe that I allowed myself to get so distracted and take my eye off the ball. Consequently, I made choices and did things that not only affected myself but the nearest and dearest to me. This was the space in jail where depression could have grown. But here is what sustained me: if the thing that has had the biggest consequences in my life are my own actions and not somebody else's then, even in this dark place called jail, there was still hope. Not so much hope really, but almost a guarantee. I could change my mind, think better, not be so angry and negative. Just like things in the past, the thing that would influence my new course the most would be me. So my world could be as I wanted it again. Realising that I had a choice was a liberating experience. I hadn't realised that focusing on the outside world – they did this, he did that – was my way of playing the victim. A childhood phrase comes back to me that seems to corroborate what I was thinking, and it goes like this: if you want to see your biggest victimiser, look in the mirror. I never imagined that those words had such truth in them. Right here, I had learned that I was my biggest victimiser. I remember sitting at the end of the bed in my cell, taking it all in. It was hard at first to accept, but there was a feeling of relief, I was in charge, I had always been in charge, but until now I had not been taking on all of the responsibility.

Without a doubt, I made the wrong choices. The ones in cricket, I am happy to see them as part of my adventure and, as I've said before, I only wish that I could have enjoyed it more with a smile on my face. Importing drugs, on the other hand, was just wrong. I don't offer up excuses for it, but in writing these words, I hope that there will be a little bit of understanding about how such bad decisions could be made. The story I would like to tell is not a drug smuggler's tale, but of someone who got himself into a position where any sort of good decision would have been hard to make. I suppose if I had been working in the City, at my weakest of moments I might have tried some financial fraud. That is not to cast aspersions on anyone, just to point out that from a bad state, bad decisions are made everywhere.

After my release, I was excited, almost as excited as that 17-year-old who went off to Leicestershire for the first time. I now inhabit a new world, one that doesn't seem as threatening, one that I can smile at, one that still contains all my hopes and aspirations – but with one big change. I don't *hope* that I can do it all, I *know* I can do it all. This isn't an attempt at being arrogant, but to let you know that we all have that capability inside of us.

It's funny, after all this time and after all that has gone on, finally it's turning around into a positive story, one in which I can still achieve my greatest dreams. Although in time those dreams have changed, I *am* still dreaming. One thing I know is that dreams do come true, and that the most powerful force that allows that to happen is yourself. If I could teach anything, I would teach this. Always look on the bright side of life – it keeps you mentally healthy. If I could bottle it, that's what I would sell. Do not take your problems too seriously, for that only seems to make them bigger in your mind, and if you make them big enough you may just end up cornering yourself.

Of course, the question 'who is the real Chris Lewis?' will be answered in actions rather than words: I choose to add more to my community, and never to make it lesser again.

16

WHO IS THE REAL CHRIS LEWIS? PART 2 – THE VIEW OF THE GHOSTWRITER

Working with Chris on and off for eighteen months or more, trying to get his story right, has been an interesting and at times challenging experience, and one which has made me question some of the decisions I have made in my own life. How easy it would have been, given different circumstances, for me to have made the same disastrous decisions that he made. That's something I have thought about a lot. Spending hour after hour writing, rewriting and then rewriting again, listening to stories from Chris's life has certainly had an impact on me.

Let me say, first, that this book is a very honest one. Chris is not the kind of man who says anything lightly. He thinks very carefully about everything and this has taken several drafts to get right. Indeed, the process was so laboured at times that I managed to write another book in the meantime. For me, it has been a wonderful experience, largely because it brought me back to being with Chris, a lad who was one of my very best friends when I was a young man.

I first met Chris at the start of his second season with Leicestershire, in my first job after leaving university and spending a year in Canada and America wondering what to do with my life. I became the county's cricket call man, which meant that I commentated on every day's play of that summer. It was the season in which Chris started in dramatic style, with wickets against the Oxford Students and Derbyshire. He immediately looked like an England player to me. He will hate me for saying it, but his awesome athleticism made him stand out from the rest. I didn't say it was natural, or that he hadn't worked on it, just that he did stand out from the rest.

Within days I wanted to get to know him – he intrigued me – and it wasn't long before we realised that we had something in common. We both saw a day's play as a job and once that was done it was time to do something else. A lot of time was spent on the road, Chris staying in the team hotel and me trying to find the cheapest dives – perhaps a dirty B&B – where I could get my head down after a night out. Having commentated all day on the team's exploits and loving every minute of it, I wanted to get away from the team, many of whom wanted to run through the day's play, sometimes ball-by-ball, over dinner.

As a journalist starting in the 1980s, I naturally liked a drink and with Chris not touching alcohol he became my driver for regular nights out, most of which ended up in a nightclub. Also as a journalist, I naturally couldn't dance. Forget about having two left feet – I didn't even have one! We would generally head out quite late, being two men in their early 20s who really didn't need that much sleep in order to put in a very professional shift the following day. Once in the nightclub, normally discovered by my late-night colleague, I would sit nursing several beverages at the bar while Chris would do his thing on the dance floor, with many eyes watching his every move. His exploits on the cricket pitch had brought him to my attention, but that was nothing compared to some of the moves he would come up with under the flashing lights in the early hours of the morning. We both had similar tastes in dance music, but while he would create quite a scene on the floor, I would gently move from side to side on my bar stool.

It never occurred to me that he was in any way different to his Leicestershire teammates; just someone who knew what he liked to do in his down time, just as I was doing, leaving my commentary colleagues behind to watch the TV or down a few brown ales in the boozer. I never concerned myself with what was going on in the dressing room as I knew that such a place did not belong to me. While I enjoyed the company of most of the players, especially Winston Benjamin, George Ferris, Tim Boon, Alan Mullally, I knew that it was not really my place to do anything other than socialise with them, apart from conducting the odd interview.

Unlike Chris, I *did* like pubs – very much, in fact – but after testing out a few I was then ready to head out for some fun. Thus, a strong bond was formed before we went our separate ways after two seasons; Chris going on to wonderful things with England, while I moved into the world of radio, TV and the *Daily Telegraph,* where I helped co-create the country's first ever newspaper fantasy football and fantasy cricket games.

I always found Chris to be funny and engaging, and in no way a difficult character or aloof, as he was often described by members of the press. There was no surprise for me when he was selected for England, but I did question some of the stories I later read in the national press about him. It seemed that some of these revealed a man who I simply didn't know. I was reading about some form of arrogance and that people didn't take to him somehow. I just didn't get that. Had he really changed that much in such a short space of time?

Working in Bristol in 2008, I was shocked when my friend Syd Lawrence, the former Gloucestershire and England bowler, called me to tell me about Chris and his arrest. We had seen each other intermittently over the years but our lives had taken us in very different directions. I could not believe what Syd was telling me. But, as it was to turn out, Chris *had* smuggled cocaine into the country. 'What's become of him?' was all I could ask. 'How could the young man with so much to offer end up in such a predicament?' What had happened to the man who was so much fun to be with?

I thought many times about visiting him in prison but, for one reason or another, I stayed away. However, like so many others, I contacted him on his release and we soon began to talk about this book. I told him that he was going to have to trust me. I'm sure he had the opportunity to work with many more established scribes than myself, but that's exactly what he did. Indeed, well before any publisher had been contacted, I sat Chris in my car, pressed record on my phone, and started to ask him questions about his arrest at Gatwick Airport. Pretty much, what you read in the first chapter of this book came from our first meeting.

While researching, I met many cricketers from the 1990s who had played against Chris and told them about the progress of this book. Many simply said that they never liked Chris, but they couldn't quite put their finger on what it was that annoyed them so. Mostly, it appeared that it was his arrogance. Hopefully, these pages have told you that that is a misconception. Confident? Yes. Wanting to do his own thing and sometimes failing to fit in? Certainly. But arrogant? No. In fact, one of the funny things about Chris is the lack of knowledge about his own statistics and performances. Constantly, I would have to remind him of his achievements. Perhaps the best example of that was when we talked about his Test debut against New Zealand. He was convinced that his first ever scalp was that of Trevor Franklin, the Kiwi opener. 'I had him caught behind,' he would try to convince me. Not according to the cricket records. Who could not remember that someone with the class of Martin Crowe was your first victim? There were plenty of examples of this.

Chris has been brutally open but not afraid to criticise the way I've written things. 'Jed, those are your words, not mine,' was often said. But it was only because he wanted this book to be an honest assessment of who he was, and is today. Chris was anything but the man he has sometimes been portrayed to be. Yes, of course, we had both changed since our younger days – him perhaps much more than me, due to his time in jail – and had lots of stories to tell each other, but we still saw in each other something that was there all those years ago.

We spent many long hours and days together as he tried to rebuild his life. In that time, it was his intelligence that shone through. Away from the work, he helped me with some personal problems, giving me some very good advice. Early on in the process, I was suffering from both depression and anxiety, and taking in information from a deep thinker who talks a lot of sense helped me greatly. I could even go as far to say that he saved my life during those turbulent times. After all, as he has explained, when the black dog attacks you, any decisions made are ones that would have made no sense at all at other times.

The whole experience over several months of working together (much of it in Chris's spare time as he needed a job to get his life back on track) was a joy.

I travelled with Chris from Nottingham, where he was living again in a small bedsit, to Llanelli in South Wales for the funeral of his first cricket mentor, Ellis Williams. He was thrilled to be asked to attend. Ten hours in the car that day offered me plenty to observe. This is a man who cares about others – he would admit to me that there is no such thing as a selfless act, that what we may think is selfless always gives us something to gain from it. He was humbled, and everyone was really pleased to see him; nobody was concerned about what he had done and the experiences through which he had recently been. He was well liked and he moved around the room effortlessly, talking to so many different people, all of whom were delighted to see him and thrilled that he had made an effort to get there.

This was the man I rediscovered while working on this book. He is not someone who sees life like others do, and the words of his mum when he was a young boy have clearly stayed with him throughout his life – that he should not follow others. This is something that governs him still.

This book has taken many different forms. Immediately, it was clear that he did not want this to be a prison diary. Indeed, it can't be one. After all, prison has only taken up a small part of his life as he approaches his 50s. There is so much more to him than that, of course. He was initially a little guarded on how he came to smuggle drugs, but in the end he did open up. This was obviously tough for him to go through. In the first newspaper interview he did after being back in normal society, Jonathan Liew from *The Daily Telegraph* wrote that Chris was cryptically guarded about his time behind bars, suggesting that he had enough mental darkness inside that he was not ready to share with anyone. I don't think that was true, although there are things that we never discussed.

At first, we dealt with nothing more than his mental state, something I have always been fascinated by. The way we act in life is not always clear to those on the outside, as they don't know what is going on inside our heads.

Once we started to talk about the drugs, I could only empathise with him. The media, and society as a whole, loves to judge and sometimes that is unfair. This is why I so wanted to write this book with Chris, because I wanted to find out what really happened to him, rather than to base my own judgement on what has been said by others. One thing became very clear early on, which was that you really can't believe everything you read or hear about someone. Chris appears to have been judged more than others, and sometimes unfairly in my opinion.

Chris did not have a normal upbringing. What he achieved as a cricketer is incredible. To come from a small area outside Georgetown, to be sent thousands of miles away to a foreign land as a young man and then face a system in the late 1970s and early 1980s when being black in the UK was not easy (remember this was the time of the riots, which began in St Paul's in Bristol before spreading through much of the rest of the country) is a remarkable achievement.

No one ever gave Chris anything as a young man. Unlike many cricketers of the time, he had not come through a public school or been spotted by coaches as a young teenager. Strength of character, a very strong will and a talent that was clearly innate but had to be worked on all the time, made him a professional cricketer.

In a society when those born with a silver spoon in their mouths are, these days, mostly mocked, the story of the rise of Chris should be applauded. What he achieved on the cricket field was something that should be used as an example to kids today. You don't need to have nice facilities at school, or to be taken to a nice club by your parents. What you need is ambition and the mental power to carry things through. And, dare I say it, some natural talent.

I was a decent cricketer when I was a teenager and had trials for Nottinghamshire. I loved the game, but I enjoyed too many other things as well and always put them before the sport. Chris did just the opposite. He put his heart and soul into cricket. It was always what he wanted to do. He uses the word 'focus' a lot.

His childhood, even in London, was never that easy. Effectively, he was an inner-city boy. These days, all the counties have community departments; their job is to use cricket as a way to take youngsters out of gangs and away from trouble (Chance to Shine is a charity which has done some remarkable work over the years in this area). Chris did not have that support. Back in the 1980s, he would have been left to his own devices. So, just the fact that he made it to Leicestershire is a terrific tale.

But then, with England always looking for the new Ian Botham, Chris was unfairly judged. His magnificent movement on a cricket pitch, I feel, sometimes made people think he was invincible. How could someone as fit as him ever be injured? How could someone with his obvious all-round talents not be scoring a hundred every other game or taking 5 wickets in every other innings? The national press, as they so often do, built him up, and whenever he didn't deliver to their standards (not Chris') he was a failure, often accused of not trying, or even of faking injury because he couldn't be bothered to play for England. This, of course, is rubbish. He was not treated the same way as some of his contemporaries, largely because of how he looked and because of his personality. He liked having an earring, driving a nice car and wearing expensive clothes − hardly the crimes of the century. Yes, he certainly made some mistakes (actually, quite a lot − Chris's own words), but who doesn't? When you are in the public eye as he was, those mistakes make many column inches.

The sport that he gave so much to eventually let him down. The evidence is now there that he spoke the truth to the ECB. Yet, given how he had been perceived nationally by the media, it was easy for them to make him the enemy. It still hurts him to this day. And, for me, there is a link between what happened to him at the end of his career and the decision he took years later to smuggle a Class A drug into the UK. At least, I think I can say with no argument that had the whole match-fixing saga not occurred, then neither would he have lost part of his life in jail. Chris received many knocks over time, many of his own doing, and if you add to that the area in north-west London he found himself in and the money worries that had escalated ever since his career ended way too early because of what he had been accused of, I hope some of you at least can understand just a little why he did what he did. I'm not trying to make excuses for him; I'm just trying to sum up how life is for some people. We are, thankfully, not all the same.

Chris is a man who wants anything other than compassion. He knows that what he did was wrong. He accepts that we all make mistakes, some much bigger than others. Hopefully, there isn't one part of his story where you think that he is looking for excuses, because he accepts that there aren't any. But, try putting yourself in his position in the autumn of 2008. Cricket was still his passion, in spite of everything, and yet his attempted comeback was ended before it had really begun. His opportunity to get back on the pitch, fill himself with much-needed confidence and put some money in his pocket, had just been snatched away from him because of injury. He is not proud of what he did, by any means. He has been open about his experiences and how they came to be. He doesn't want any sympathy – indeed, he would hate it – but I just hope this is a story which shows people that life isn't always black and white, that just because you achieve good things in life does not stop you making some major errors along the way.

This is a classic rise and fall tale, but with lots of bits in between. And happily with another rise at the end of it. Chris has worked hard on trying to get fit enough to play the game he still adores. At home, he will often get off the couch and pick up his bat or a cricket ball. It's a sport that still lives within him. And, thanks to the extraordinary efforts of Jason Ratcliffe and the PCA, he now is working so hard on ensuring that his life story – or at least part of it – is a unique one. I hope that those young cricketers he met on his tour of the county grounds last winter took something from him. I hope the reader of this does too.

Thanks so much for taking the time out to read this. I appreciate your time in doing so. I hope you have enjoyed it as much as I have working on it and maybe learned that you should never judge a book by its cover. In this case, that is literally true.

INDEX

Hulio ei hir dawelwch.

CAETH
a Rhydd

PEREDUR LYNCH

CARREG GWALCH

Er Cof am fy Rhieni

a'm Chwaer, Amranwen Haf

RHAGAIR

Hyfrydwch pur fu cael cydweithio gyda'r Prifardd Myrddin ap Dafydd a Gwasg Carreg Gwalch wrth baratoi'r gyfrol hon ar gyfer ei hargraffu. Rwy'n eithriadol o ddiolchgar i'r Cyngor Llyfrau am ei haelioni ac am y Grant Dylunio a sicrhaodd wasanaeth Olwen Fowler fel dylunydd. Roeddwn i eisoes yn edmygydd o waith Olwen, ac ar ôl cael y fraint fawr o gydweithio mor agos â hi dyfnhawyd yr edmygedd hwnnw ymhellach. Darllenodd Branwen Jarvis a Robat Trefor y testun gyda'u trylwyredd arferol ac mae'r gwaith gorffenedig yn llawer glanach yn sgil eu sylwadau gwerthfawr.

Cwblhawyd y gyfrol hon yn ystod cyfnod o seibiant ymchwil a dreuliais yn Adran Ieithoedd a Llenyddiaethau Celtaidd Prifysgol Harvard rhwng Medi a Rhagfyr 2016. Rwy'n hynod o ddiolchgar i'r Athro Catherine McKenna am estyn croeso mor dywysogaidd imi ac i'm cydletywr yn Bowdoin Street, Cambridge, Yr Athro Steve Striffler, am ei gwmnïaeth ddifyr. Cefais nawdd ariannol ar gyfer yr ymweliad o Waddoliad Yr Athro Wynn Humphrey Davies, a weinyddir ar gyfer Prifysgol Bangor gan Gwmni'r Brethynwyr. Mae fy niolch pennaf, serch hynny, i Menna, Tomos a Meilyr am ganiatáu i mi ddianc am gyfnod estynedig rhag fy nyletswyddau teuluol.

CYNNWYS

LLOCHES *

I

Mynd yn ôl

Mor rhwydd fu oedi am flwyddyn,
Rhy hawdd fu gohirio hyn
A rhoi'r lle i feinwe'r llwch
Hulio ei hir dawelwch.

Ar wae'r llynedd cau'r llenni
Yna mynd a wneuthum i
O wyll oer y 'stafell hon
A'i gadael yn gysgodion,
Ac o'i golwg, wrth gilio,
Ei throi'n ddodrefn cefn y co';
Cadw'i dysg rhag hyd y dydd
Ym mynwent fy ymennydd.

Ond ofer hyn. Dod fu raid
Dros riniog drws yr enaid;
Dod yma i ymgodymu
Â llais mud rhyw fyd a fu;
Dod adre' heb ddyhead,
A dod yn ôl i dŷ 'nhad
I durio drwy ddyfnderoedd
Y gwyll hwn. Ei lyfrgell oedd.

---

* Er cof am fy nhad, y Parchedig Evan Lynch (1917–2011), a fu'n weinidog gydag
Eglwys Bresbyteraidd Cymru yn ardaloedd Carrog, Glyndyfrdwy a Bryneglwys drwy
gydol ei yrfa.

Focs ar focs rwy'n pacio'i fyd.

Mae meingefnau amheuon
A ffydd oes ar silffoedd hon.
Er ei fynd agoraf i
Drwy ei llên amdo'r llenni
A gweld afreswm y gair
Yn un cno yn cyniwair.
Res ar res rwy'n gweld drwy'r hedd
Ymlyniad trigain mlynedd
A hen, hen faich un a fu
Yn isel was i'r Iesu.

Rwy'n ôl ymhlith llyfrau 'nhad
Am mai hyn fu'i gymyniad.
Rwy'n bodio'i go', yna'i gau.
Didol ei fyfyrdodau
A wnaf fesul llyfr hefyd.
Focs ar focs rwy'n pacio'i fyd.

II

Yr hyn sy'n aros

Ac wedi'r holl flynyddoedd
Yr hyn sy'n aros
Yw sawr orennau.

O ddydd i ddydd, yma'n ei gell gau,
Fe fyddai 'nhad
Yn ymestyn am orennau.

Pan fyddai'r tywydd ar ei dduaf
Fe fyddai ef â'i ewinedd a'i fysedd
Yn diosg y croen araul
Ac yn bendithio'r dydd â darnau o haul.

Ac ar y bwrdd o'i flaen,
Yma ymhlith ei lyfrau,
Ymhlith ei lyfrau a'i fyfyrdodau
Yr oedd o hyd groen orennau.

Yr oedd yma hefyd,
Wrth iddo saernïo ei bregethau,
Ryw flas rhwng surni a melystra
Ar daflod ei fyd.

Ac wrth ddod yn ôl i bacio'i lyfrau,
Ar ôl yr holl flynyddoedd
Yr hyn sy'n aros
Yw sawr orennau.

Coleg y Bala, 1945

Eiliad yw'r hyn a welaf.
Llun yw hwn sy'n llawn o haf
A haul eu tymor olaf.

Egwyl wen heb gysgod glaw.
Ond yr oedd sŵn rhyfel draw
I'w heulwen yn gyfalaw.

Eiliad a ddifrifolwyd
Sy'n y llun. Drwy'r siwtiau llwyd
Eu heiddilwch a ddaliwyd.

Ai Ef a'u galwodd ynghyd
O erwau'r cawn a'r cae ŷd?
O'r lofa a'r chwarel hefyd?

Rhoi Ei hawl ar feidrolion,
Ac ym mrad yr eiliad hon
Eu dwyn i achub dynion.

Rhoi gair mor ddi-ddal â'r gwynt
Yn waddol gyrfa iddynt
A'u hel heb 'sgrepan i'w hynt.

Eu hel a'r byd yn chwalu
Fom wrth fom, a'r sicrwydd fu
Yno'n datod o'u deutu.

IV

Esgyn i'r mynydd*

O'r mynydd, meddai, y dôi ei gymorth,
Ac ar ei daith eciwmenaidd drwy'r coed
Yr oedd unwaith ddelwau
Yn rhoi amlinell i'w fyfyrdodau.

Simon o Gyrene yn dwyn baich ei Arglwydd,
Gwragedd Jerwsalem yn galaru:
Roedd holl orsafau'r dioddefaint yno
A llwybr yn ymestyn
At dair croes ar fryn fry.

Ond aeth y delwau un dydd,
Mynd mor llwyr ag arogldarth ddoe
A'i adael ef yno yn y pin tywyllddu.

Ac eto, dod yn ôl o hyd a wnâi.
Dwyn pwn y dydd drwy'r coed caeadfrig,
Dyrchafu'i lygaid fry gan adael llyfr a dysg o'i ôl,
Camu'n ddi-lithr drwy'r bwlch i'r mynydd
Lle nad oedd ond tair croes yn pydru.

Ac oddi yno, meddai, y dôi ei gymorth.
Yno, lle ciliai'r holl gysgodion,
Yr oedd yr awel, meddai, yn ysgafnach,
Yn troelli'n beraidd fel y mynnai.
Ac yno, dros y bryniau pell, fe welai weithiau wlad Gilead
A newydd fyd yn tarddu allan yn y dyffryn.

---

* Yn 1948 agorwyd coleg cenhadol gan y Catholigion mewn plasty ar gyrion Carrog.
Mewn coedlan gerllaw codwyd delwau ar lun Gorsafoedd y Groes, a thair croes bren
ar y foel agored y tu hwnt i'r coed. Caewyd y coleg yn ystod y 1970au a symudwyd y
delwau, gan adael y tair croes i araf bydru dros y blynyddoedd. Yn ddyddiol bron byddai
fy nhad yn cerdded y llwybr hwn.

V Encilio

Weithiau byddai'r dyddiau du — 'n ei hawlio
A hen niwl yn lledu;
Yntau 'mhlith ei lyfrau lu
'Godai wal rhag ei deulu.

Ni yrrai o'r dyfnderoedd — unrhyw air.
Yno rhwng y silffoedd
Bolltau ar eiriau a oedd
A mudan pendrwm ydoedd.

Nid oedd wrth gyfrif dyddiau — ei hir faich
Unrhyw falm i'w glwyfau
Na iaith in i esmwytháu
Na deall ei bydewau.

Ai'r un ing a lithrai'n ôl — yno i'w gell
Yn ei gylch tymhorol?
A ddôi yno'i orffennol
A hen gam yn saeth drwy'i gôl?

A welai'i fam yn gwaelu? — A welai
Yr aelwyd yn chwalu?
Oedd o yno'n cwmanu
Dan faich y cariad na fu?

Ond âi o hyd y pwn du, — o'i niwloedd
Fe'i gwelem yn camu;
Fe wawriai'r haul eto fry
A dôi eilwaith at deulu.

VI

Methu esbonio'r Drefn

Â lôn neb y bore bach
Y mae'n gyfarwydd mwyach.
Yn llwydolau dechrau'r dydd
Mae o'n hawlio'r heolydd.
Daw rhyddid y wawr iddo
Ac yn nhân ei injan o
Mae her ddwys ei ymryddhad.
Yn ei holew'n pystylad
Y mae mil o garnau meirch . . .

Tro . . .
  Sgrech teiars . . .
    Gwrych . . .
      Tyweirch . . .
Eiliad a gwaedd anaele
Darn o oes rhwng daer a ne'.
Dur a gwydr ac adwy
A mab nad yw yno mwy . . .

Sŵn clecian tân yn tynnu,
Rhu Chwefror oer a'i awch fry.
Mae'n wynt. Ond yma mae 'nhad.
Yma i'w lên mae'i ymlyniad.

A'r gaea'n taro'i gawell,
Yma mae y storm ymhell.
Fan hyn ymestyn y mae
Dilyniant y dalennau;
Ei lyfrau'n sgaffaldiau'i ffydd
A rhin geiriau yn geyrydd.

A'i abwyd drwy'r anwybod,
Y pnawn hwn fe wn ei fod
Yn dyheu am blwc o'r dŵr,
Yno'n chwennych â'i chynnwr'
Ennyd o weld ar bnawn du.

Yna mae'r ffôn yn canu
Ac mae angau dechrau'r dydd
Yn rhodio drwy'r parwydydd,
A'i geyrydd sy'n ysgyrion
Yma 'mrad yr eiliad hon . . .

Yn ias yr hwyr mynd sy raid
Draw heno at drueiniaid;
Tanio'i gar eto'n y gwyll,
Dilyn Duw y lôn dywyll;
O gêr i gêr gyrru'n gall
I ddüwch dyfna'i ddeall.

O ddyffryn pob anobaith
I'w dywys ef nid oes iaith,
Na llais yn ehangder llwm
Y rhos lle derfydd rheswm.
Y nos hon nid oes yno
Ond griddfan ei injan o
Yn troi, troi olwynion tranc,
Yn rhofio bedd i'r ifanc.

Yna o'i flaen fe wêl ef
Dyddyn ar fryn dioddef,
A dau dlawd, hen ŷd y wlad,
A'u hwyrnos yn alarnad,
Dau glòs, diymffrost eu hynt,
Dau â dyrnod ffawd arnynt.

I gegin pob anobaith
Mae'n dod â mudandod iaith.
Gwae, gennad Duw! Gwae, gnawd dall!
Fe ddaw heb fodd o ddeall
Na gair ym mhlygion ei go'
I'w harwain a'u cysuro.
Ond ei ran yw dod o raid
I rannu noethni'r enaid;
Dod o'r hwyr, troi'r ddau yn dri,
A rhannu'r holl drueni;
Dod gan droedio drwy'r adwy
I dŷ mab nad yw'n bod mwy.

VII

Setiau radio'r ugeinfed ganrif

Fan hyn ar derfyn dydd fe fyddai 'nhad yn gwrando
Ar y radio. O hwyr i hwyr tu ôl i'r drws caeedig hwn
Dôi cymesuredd tôn a choethder llais y BBC
Â chwrs y byd i gyd i'w gell. Fflach gwn ger Pont ar Ddyfi.
Hillsborough. Soweto. Suez. Y cloddio dreng
Ar rostir yn Swydd Efrog draw. Mewn cystrawennau cain y
                                                              daeth
Enbydrwydd y blynyddoedd i'r ystafell hon.

A minnau, wrth i mi'n blentyn lithro i ddyfnderoedd cwsg,
Fe glywn i weithiau isel rŵn y radio. Ymchwydd a thrai
                                                              brawddegau
Yn pellhau o hyd. Ni wyddwn i fod holl lywiawdwyr daear
Yma yng nghell fy nhad. De Gaulle, Nixon, Brandt a
                                                              Brezhnev:
Buont oll yma yn lloffa ymhlith y llyfrau.
Digwyddodd y cyfan fan hyn. Fan hyn oedd Nuremburg
A Srebrenica. Fan hyn oedd Biaffra a Zeebrugge.
Fan hyn ym mil naw saith deg tri y pallodd llif yr olew.
Fan hyn oedd Dealey Plaza. Yma, o storfa lên y chweched silff
Y taniwyd yr ergydion. Chwalodd penglog Kennedy fan hyn
A phlastrwyd darnau o'i ymennydd ar ôl-rifynnau'r *Faner*.
Fan hyn, un bore Gwener, o grombil dysg a diwinyddiaeth,
Y llithrodd tomen Merthyr Vale. Gwacawyd llyfrau o'u
                                                              hystyron.
Llifodd tunelli'r geiriau oddi ar eu tudalennau
A throdd eu print yn slwj du yn ffroenau ac yng ngyddfau
                                                              plant.

Fan hyn ar derfyn dydd fe fyddai 'nhad yn gwrando
Ar y radio. Ac ar ôl ei fynd fe'u cesglais hwy ynghyd.
Cyrchu hen setiau radio o'r llofftydd ac o'r atic.
Bush, Roberts, Grundig, Hitachi: yma ar y bwrdd o'm blaen
Fe welaf i yn awr ymdaith technoleg tonfeddi'r awyr.

Ond ni ddaw un smic ohonynt mwyach.
Mae'r lleisiau a oedd ynddynt wedi mynd.
Ceulodd trigain mlynedd o waed yn y falfiau.
Diferodd bustl y byd o'r batris, a throdd dagrau hallt
Gweddwon a phlant yr holl wifrau'n llwch.
A thrwy berfeddion tywyll eu gwneuthuriad,
Trwy ddargludyddion a thransistorau bu'r brain yn tyllu,
Yn tyllu, tyllu wrth ysglyfaethu briwgig canrif.

Fan hyn ar derfyn dydd fe fyddai 'nhad yn gwrando
Ar y radio. A rhywsut, ar ôl ei ddiffodd, yr oedd o'n dal
                              i fentro credu,
Yn betio eto mai Duw cariad yw.

VIII

Y gell olaf

Yno roedd o wedi'i ddal, — cadwynau
 Ein gwenau'n ei gynnal;
 Iddo rhoed penyd meddal
 Byd yr hen a'i bedair wal.

Tameidiau o adnodau'n dod — o'i fin
 A'i fyd yn grebachdod;
 Er rhoi llef hir â'i holl fod,
 Dywedwst oedd y Duwdod.

Ei enaid yn newynu, — yna'i iaith
 Ei hun yn ei wadu;
 Cystrawennau'i lyfrau lu
 Fel ei lên yn diflannu.

Ac i'w gynnal â'm gwenau — yno'r awn,
 Ond yn nhro'r munudau
 Roedd dyfnderoedd dieiriau,
 Hen, hen dawch rhyngom ein dau.

A welai'r fuddugoliaeth? — Ni wn i.
 Cans yn nhymp marwolaeth
 Un hawl sydd i'r ddynoliaeth:
 Yn fud at fud ef a aeth.

Un nos hir fe'i gwyliais o — o efyn
 Pob gofal yn llithro,
 Yn gwrhau i bridd a gro
 A dirni'r cread arno.

IX

Yn y pwll nofio

Ai am hyn y bu'n ymholi yn y tir tywyll?
Ai peth fel hyn ydi o?
Plymio i'r dyfnder fel hyn
A'r dŵr clir yn llosgi'r llygaid.
Yna dallineb ennyd,
Llonyddwch baban mewn croth
O dan y môr o wydr.

Y codi oddi yno i'r wyneb;
Ai peth fel hyn ydi o?
Yr ymladd dygn am anadl
Cyn dod trwy gynnwrf y dyfroedd
A phlant yn diasbedain ar bob tu.

Ac yna awr yr ymegnïo.
Cyhyrau'n ymgodymu â dŵr,
Ysgyfaint yn ymgodymu â chyhyrau
A'r dŵr clir yn golchi'r beiau.
Y noethni wedyn mewn ymolchfa
A'r gawod fywiol ar fy ngwegil
Yn llawn fel lli.

Ai peth mor syml â hyn ydi o?
Plymio i'r dyfnder fel hyn a chamu oddi yma
Yn newydd-anedig i'r dydd?

X Trefnu llyfrau

Ei lyfrau rhagor fydd piau'i stori
A'u hawlio o'i annedd a wnes eleni.
Y mae ei alwad a'i holl ymholi,
Mae'r cyfan yma'n focseidiau imi.
I'w roi 'mhlith fy llyfrau i, — yma'n ôl
Fe ddois â gwaddol ei ddysg a'i weddi.

Af ati i'w gosod. Ei fyfyrdodau
A'i einioes ydyw yr holl reseidiau.
Mae'i ddwylo yno drwy'r holl ddalennau
A'i fywyd rhywsut ym mhrint yr oesau,
Ac yn nhrefn y meingefnau — mae'i fyd o
Yn hawlio heno fy silffoedd innau.

AR FEDD FY MAM
(1925 – 81)

Fe'i ceid lle'r oedd direidi, — hon welid
Lle'r oedd sêl yn cyfri';
Un oedd y wên a'r weddi,
Un ei chân a'i hymdrech hi.

AR FEDD AMRANWEN HAF
(1955 – 2003)

Ni weddai mo henaint iddi — na chrych
Ar wedd na dihoeni;
Fan hyn, pan ddaw'n penwynni,
Ni chawn ond ei harddwch hi.

AR FEDD FY NAIN
(1899 – 1980)

Er trymed yw'r nos drosti, — ni all arch
Mwy na'r llwch 'roed arni
Na daear ei distewi;
Yn y cof di-dranc yw hi.

I'R ATHRO
R. GERAINT GRUFFYDD
AR EI YMDDEOLIAD

Mae dyfnder, mae llawnder lliw — dydd o haf
   Yn dy ddysg ddiledryw,
   Canys clared aeddfed yw,
   Gwin i hudo'r gwan ydyw.

Fel ffrwyth glân dy winllan di — heneiddio'n
   Fonheddig foed iti,
   A pharhau i rannu'n ffri
   Haul euraid dy seleri.

O oes i oes un Eglwys sydd.
Hen ywt Tragwyddol newydd!

Ei Eglwys Ef ywr gwagle.

DATHLU DENGMLWYDDIANT CAPEL BEREA NEWYDD, BANGOR 2003-2013

Yn Nhŷ Cwrdd Tywysog Hedd
Un anadl yw deng mlynedd.
Ein hadeilad, eiliad yw,
A dinodedd dyn ydyw.
Un eiliad ydyw'r waliau,
Byr yw oes eu morter brau.

Ond a'n gweddi'n llenwi'r lle,
Ei Eglwys Ef yw'r gwagle.
Yno o dan ei thrawstiau hi,
Yno o fewn ei phriddfeini
Y ceir holl ganrifoedd cred
A moroedd pob ymwared.

Mae'r awel ym Merea
Heno'n dwyn newyddion da.
Hir yw ei balm, a thra bo
Yma un yn amenio
A llaw Iôr ar y lle hwn,
Nid adeilad a welwn.

O oes i oes un Eglwys sydd.
Hen yw! Tragwyddol newydd!
Hi yw gwledd y gwagle hwn,
Hi a saif lle'i deisyfwn
Yn barhad mewn morter brau,
Yn fawr rhwng cyfyng furiau.

IWAN

Mae sôn bod meibion y mans
O oes i oes yn niwsans.
O blwyf i blwyf maent yn bla
A'u hawl yw gwrthryfela.

Eu hawl hwy yw dod i'r wledd
Yn filain eu gorfoledd,
A rhoi her â'u chwerthin rhwydd
Yn oriau'r dwys ddistawrwydd.

Wedi awr dy angau di
Arhoswn yn y tresi.
Aeth glewder ein menter mwy
Yn lewder anweladwy.
Tir llwyd diantur yw llên,
Tŷ taeog yw tŷ awen.
Ein rhan yw dilyn yr haid
A gollwng cledd y gwylliaid.
Y reddf yw byw a gwrhau,
Anwylwn ein hualau!

Ond ni all dyrnod y ne'
Hawlio dy gân i geule.
Ni all un teyrn ei dryllio
Na chloi cerdd na chwalu co'
Am steddfodau'r dyddiau da,
Na hawlio'r rebel ola'.

Yn daer, yn driw, byddi di,
Yn anniddig dy weddi,
Yn fardd o Fynwy i Fôn,
Yn hyfrydlais afradlon,
Yr her iach, yn chwerthin rhwydd
Yn oriau'r dwys ddistawrwydd.

MARW DIC JONES

Tra bo dynoliaeth fe fydd hiraethu
A phen i dalar a phoen i deulu.
I wlad daw eiliad i ymdawelu,
I hendre a loriwyd daw hir alaru,
A bydd, fel erioed y bu, — gau dorau
Ar gnydau'r hafau a'r cynaeafu.

Ond tra bo tafod, sillaf a nodau
A rhywrai'n cywain ein llên o'r caeau,
Bydd dawn yn aros, bydd dyn a'i eiriau
A chân o'i hyngan yn drech nag angau.
Bydd huodledd, bydd awdlau — a stori
Yno ym miri y pentymhorau.

GWENLLIAN

Ni welaist, ferch, mo'r eiliad,
Ni welaist ti loes dy dad
Na'r bicell yn sgrafellu'n
Rhwyll ei ben, na'r dur lle bu
Yr holl ewynnau ar waith
A'i ymennydd llym unwaith.

Tu hwnt i'n gwaedd oeddet ti,
Ni wyddet ing ein gweddi;
Tu hwnt i'n dolef hefyd
A'n dagrau oll yn dy grud;
I'n diodde' diddeall,
I waed y wawr plentyn dall.

A thrwy'r gaeaf olaf un
Ni welaist warchae'r gelyn,
Na'i feirch o Fuellt i Fôn,
Na llwydwyll ein colledion,
Na dawns y pedolau'n dwyn
I Wynedd dristwch gwanwyn.

Yna dy roi'n y côr draw
I eilio siant ac alaw;
Rhoi i Fair pob her a fu
A'n hundod mewn lleiandy;
Rhoi i'r Iôn ein sofraniaeth,
Yno i Dduw rhoi'r ha' na ddaeth.

Ynot hyd dy benwynni
Roedd gwlad a'i dyhead hi;
Ynot ein breuddwyd ninnau
Ac ogof wag ein gwasgfâu;
Ac yn dy gnawd gwyn o hyd
Roedd haf anghyrraedd hefyd.

Ni welaist, ferch, mo'r eiliad,
Ni welaist ti loes dy dad,
Eto'i waed oedd ynot ti,
Ei hen urddas yn corddi;
Ynot ei holl sofraniaeth,
Yn dy fru ei Gymru'n gaeth.

COFIO LLYWELYN YN 1982

O'n cof taer fe'i cafwyd, do, — un ing mawr,
    Deuddeng mis ohono;
    Eirias drist fu'n cân dros dro
    Nes i alar noswylio.

Lle bu dafnau d'angau di — yn rhoi lliw
    Ar dir llwm Cilmeri,
    Am un nawn fe aethom ni
    Â'n hystyriol dosturi.

Un orig o filwrio, — un orig
    O ail-fyw'r hen gyffro
    A daniodd dy waed yno,
    Un awr o her yn ein tro.

Herio, a dim ond geiriau — yn rhoi awch
    Fel erioed i'n harfau;
    Â'n llefain oll eu llyfnhau,
    Eu hogi â'n brawddegau.

Roedd wylo'n rhwydd am flwyddyn, — ein mawrhad
    'Run mor hawdd, Lywelyn;
    Geiriau gwag hyd Ragfyr gwyn,
    Yna d'adael di wedyn.

GWYLAN

Roedd craith i'w gweled neithiwr
Yn hollti'r don, lledu'r dŵr,
A'i hystaen fel dawns o dân
Yn lliwio'r môr a'r marian.

Crio llesg o graig gerllaw;
Âi gwylan gryg ei halaw
Uwch dwndwr y dŵr di-hid
Gan gyhwfan mewn gofid.

Wylai a fflam drwy'r dyli,
Fe wylai tra llosgai'r lli;
Un chwa o ing oedd ei chân,
Un gri eofn drwy'r graean.

Fe fu'r môr ar dân ganwaith,
Bu hithau am oesau maith
Yn naddu â llais eiddil
Fin nos ar feddfaen ei hil.

Un wylan fel pe'n gwylio'r
Gwrym mawr a agorai'r môr;
Ei wylio cyn ildio'n ôl,
Hedeg at graig gysgodol.

Mae Heledd yma eilwaith,
Mae merch y gofidiau maith
Yn dal i siarad o hyd,
I lefain drwy'r glaw hefyd.

CYWYDD CROESAWU
EISTEDDFOD YR URDD
I FRO GLYNDŴR, 1993

A'r drin yn rhy daer inni
A chno'n hofn yn drech na ni,
O'r tir hwn, o Gymru'r tranc
Nid yw yn anodd dianc.
Rhag penyd yr ennyd hon
Ein rhyddhad yw'n breuddwydion.

Yn nhir ein breuddwydion ni
Mae'r hil yn ymwroli,
Ac Owain, Owain a'i wŷr
A welwn. Mae sŵn milwyr
Yn nesu drwy y noswynt
Cyn cilio eto i'w hynt.

Rhag gwasgfâu hwyrnosau'n hiaith
Oni welwn ni eilwaith
Yn nharth ein dychmygion ni
Y glew a'u harfau'n gloywi,
A'r meirch yn yr oriau mân,
A'n draig a'n mab darogan?

Er rhyddhad ein breuddwydion,
Trech o hyd yw'r ennyd hon.
Ni ddaw byddinoedd Owain
Na'i arwyr ef, llwch yw'r rhain.
Meirwon pob un ohonynt,
Mân ronynnau'n gwau'n y gwynt.

O raid yr â'r dewr i'r drin,
A ni heddiw yw'r fyddin!
Ni yw'r caneuon ieuanc,
Arwyr triw yng Nghymru'r tranc;
Yn oriau'i hing, ni yw'r hwyl,
Ni'r her yn nhir ei harwyl.

I gaeau dawns ac awen
Fe dry'r llu, at lwyfan llên.
Yno i'r blaen, dewch, henwyr blin,
A chewch wyrth chwyldro ein chwerthin,
A throir Mai a pherthi'r mêl
Â'n hafiaith yn wrthryfel.

Ond hyd yr elôn hen
Yn nirfawr angau angen,
Bydd y t'wysog yn cofio
Am y stôr a gwres y croeso.

ARRESTS IN BANGOR

THE BANGOR
AND NORTH WALES
WEEKLY NEW

THURSDAY, OCTOBER 29, 1981

...ood route chosen for first winter outing

Seven in court after incidents during Royal visi...

By
Dafydd V. Jones and
David Greenwood

Flag-waving welcome dims chants of student protest

BANGOR 1981-5

Nid gwŷr a drigai ym Mangor yn y dyddiau hynny,
O na, roedd arwyr yr Hen Ogledd yno'n fyw;
Meibion Godebog, Tudfwlch Hir fab Cilydd,
Ac yr oedd Urien Rheged yno'n rhywle 'mysg y criw.

Ac yng nghilfachau'r Globe, y Menai Vaults a'r Buckley
Nid mân feidrolion oedd yn tynnu'r pympiau chwaith.
Ynddynt yr oedd Mynyddog Mwynfawr yn ymrithio
Ac yn y Taj Mahal ai Cwmbreg oedd yr iaith?

Roedd Allt Glanrafon hithau yn Fynydd Bannog
A dŵr Derwennydd yn y Fenai'n wyn.
Ond och, yr oeddynt hwythau, hen ddihirod Deifr
                                    a Brynaich,
A Fflamddwyn hefyd yn ei Goleg ar y Bryn.

✳

Gwŷr aeth i Fangor, hyderus eu cam,
Glân eu magwraeth ar aelwydydd di-nam.
Ar ddirwest y'u maged yn yr ysgol Sul,
Dadl ddiau yw iddynt ymadael â'r hen lwybr cul.

Gwrgi'r parablwr o diroedd y de,
Mewn rhuthr am y bar nid ildiai ei le.
Am bynciau difrifddwys hyd oriau'r bore
Taer y taerai wrth roi'r byd yn ei le.

Cynon fab Clydno o henfro'r chwareli,
Staenedig ei ddenims ymhob parti.
Llawer merch ar ei ôl yn ymholi,
Llawer deigr o'i achos yn cronni.

Owain gerdd-dantiwr o bau Llanuwchllyn,
Uwch gwegi'r dafarn parod â'i emyn.
Heb nacáu fe roddodd ym mrwydrau'r ewyn
I gigfrain Bangor ddiwylliant Penllyn.

Yntau Aneirin o gwmwd Edeirnion,
Cynt y pydrai mewn gwely cysurlon
Na throi i lyfrgell y llyfrau trymion,
Gelyn diysgog y boreau prydlon.

※

Brynhawn dydd Iau protest fawr a fu.
Ymgynullodd myfyrwyr Bangor yn bedwar llu
Ger neuadd y ddinas. Ac fel hyn y bu.
Daeth tywysog hefo'i wraig mewn Rolls-Royce du
Ac o'i weled dyrchafwyd bomiau drewdod a'u taflu
Yn arogldarth o'i flaen, a rhyddhawyd cadlef hy
Am 'frad un dau wyth dau' cyn cyrraedd o'r heddlu
Fel tonnau tost eu gwaedd i ysgyrnygu.

A bu herio taer ac ymwthio o bob tu,
A cholli limpyn a charchar gyrchu
A dirfawr ddewrder cyn i'r cops lwyr drechu.
Ond hyd yr elo'n hen
Yn nirfawr angau angen,
Bydd y t'wysog yn cofio
Am y stŵr a gwres y croeso.

※

Mae'r gwŷr gwrdd fu 'Mangor gynt
A'u hyder? Ai meirw ydynt?
Mae'r her oedd i'w miri hwy
A hen rwymau eu tramwy?

Piau'r bedd o dan ddrysi
Y llogau a'r morgeisi?
Bedd parablwr, bedd Gwrgi.

Piau'r bedd yng Nghaernarfon
Draw yn stiwdio'i ofalon?
Bedd partïwr, bedd Cynon.

Piau'r bedd yng nglan y llyn
Yn y gwersyll sy 'Mhenllyn?
Bedd Owain daer ei emyn.

Piau'r bedd ymysg manion
Academaidd fanylion?
Bedd y bardd o Edeirnion.

Ond er hyn ni ddarfu'r ias
A fu gynt i'w cymdeithas.
Ar hwyrnosau hiraethlon
Fe fydd byw'r gwŷr o galon,
A bydd angerdd ieuenctid
Yn y co'n ddigyfnewid,
A bydd gwefr ac atgofion
Uwch y bîr a'r gwydrau gloywon
A gwŷr ifanc Mynyddog
Yn dragwyddol ddiysgog.

HANESYDD

Doeddwn i ddim yn ei nabod o,
Ond fe fyddai'n ddi-ffael yn fy nghyfarch â gwên
A d'wedai pawb mai gŵr bonheddig oedd.

Weithiau fe'i gwelwn ar nosweithiau llaith
Yn mynd o'i waith i wyll y ddinas,
Ac mewn rhyw faestref draw
Gwyddwn y byddai tan yr oriau mân
Yno'n cribinio'i fyrdd nodiadau.

Gwyddwn y byddai wrthi'n darllen
Am drasiedïau a llofruddiaethau,
Am forynion a dreisiwyd a babanod a foddwyd.
Ac o hyn, mi wyddwn, fe luniai lyfrau,
A thrwy'i ddyfalwch tosturiol fe greai gampweithiau
Am enbyd rawd yr isel rai yng ngwlad y menyg gwynion.

A dyma glywed flynyddoedd wedyn am sydynrwydd
                                        ei fynd,
Nad oedd un gobaith iddo
A bod y cancr ymhobman drwyddo,
Ac fel y bu i'r hen gydymaith tywyll,
Trwy hir nosweithiau'i ymchwil dyfal,
Yn ddistaw, ddistaw ei hawlio yntau
Â'r un dyfalwch.

Peth felly'n ddi-au yw ysgolheictod angau.

WEDI'R ANGLADD

Ac wrth iddyn nhw ddod oddi yno
Dyma nhw'n dweud y byddai hi byw,
Y byddai parhad i'w harddwch hi yng ngwedd y plant
Ac y byddai angau'n ddiarglwyddiaeth
A heb golyn mwyach.

Ond yr oedd hynny flynyddoedd mawr yn ôl.
Cans yn yr oriau mân, a'r ddinas ddu yn cysgu,
Wrth iddo lyncu gwaddod ola'r dydd,
Wrth fodio'i ffordd drwy holl sianeli'r nos,
Y mae o'n gwybod yn amgenach.

Yno, wrth glywed sŵn seirenau'n mynd a dod,
Mi fydd o'n gweld yn sgrin ei ben
Nad yw'r hen angau'n ddiarglwyddiaeth,
Ac yno, weithiau,
Mi fydd o'n teimlo'i golyn enbyd yn ei fron.

I TONY BLAIR – CROESGADWR IRAC – AR EI YMDDEOLIAD

Ymhob rhyw wlad pan siarado, — ni waeth
Pa mor hen y byddo,
Drwy y wên or-daer honno
Daw y gwaed o hyd i go'.

CERDDORFA

Wrth i gordiau doniau dyn — ruthro i'w hynt,
Wrth i'r wefr droi'n ddeigryn,
Gwn fod y Duwdod ei hun
Â'i law yno ar linyn.

MEWN DAU GAE

I ddau barc fe ddaw y byd, — a daw'r awr
    Pan dry'r waun drom hefyd
    A'i henfaes yn gyfanfyd,
    Dau gae yn gread i gyd.

I GYFARCH
JOHN LLYWELYN WILLIAMS *

Gofal nid llety a gafwyd, — dy afiaith
    Nid 'stafell a brofwyd,
    Annedd lon nid neuadd lwyd,
    Nid adeilad ond aelwyd.

---

* Ar ei ymddeoliad fel Warden Neuadd John Morris-Jones, Prifysgol Bangor.

HIRAETH

Ynom o hyd yn gof maith — mae deigryn
Sydd yn hŷn na'n heniaith;
Rhyw ddistyll o'r llwydwyll llaith
A'n lluniodd ni oll unwaith.

CRI'R YMADAWEDIG

Ni fynnaf eich griddfannau; — ni hawliaf
Dorcalon, 'rhen ffrindiau;
Dewch yma i gofio'r oriau
Llawn a oedd a llawenhau.

GWYMON

Ar draeth y cenedlaethau, — wedi i ni
Droi'n un â'r pellterau,
A fwrir rhith llipa frau
Ohonom gan y tonnau?

EWYN

A'r don yn deilchion, heno daeth — o'r môr
Furmuron llawn hiraeth,
Ac yn ôl drwy'r cregyn aeth
Un eiliad o'n bodolaeth.

Ac yn ôl drwy'r cregyn aeth

Un eiliad o'n bodolaeth.

PLENTYN

Eiliad ar draeth hirfelyn — yw dy hwyl
Cyn i'r don oresgyn
Yn y gwyll dy gestyll gwyn
A hen wae yn ei hewyn.

DAWNS FLODAU

Eiddil ŷnt yng ngŵydd y wlad, — yn eu plyg
Dim ond plant am eiliad
Ar grindir ein hir barhad
Yn rhoi ias i'n goroesiad.

I ALIS HAF
YN UN AR HUGAIN OED

I'th hwyliau nerth a hawliaf, — a haul Awst
Ar dy lwybr a fynnaf,
A hefyd fe ddeisyfaf
Dy les o hyd, Alis Haf.

I SARAN LYNCH
AM ENNILL GRADD
YN Y GYMRAEG

Heddiw yn dy gyrhaeddiad — y mae mwy
    Na marc a dosbarthiad;
    Yn dy lwydd mae llên dy wlad,
    Yn dy radd dy wareiddiad.

I LOIS ANGHARAD
YN 18 OED

A'r lluwch cyn uched â'r lloer — yn ein byd
    A'r mis bach mor iasoer
    A'i law hefyd yn lafoer,
    Hon yw'r haul bob Chwefror oer.

A'n gaea' hir inni'n gŵyn, — hon yw'r balm
    Ry' ben ar ein hachwyn,
    Yn sŵn ei dawns hon sy'n dwyn
    Rin a hoen rhyw hen wanwyn.

CIG OEN ORGANIG Y RUG

Gwair a meillion yn donnau, — a dolydd
Dihalog. Perlysiau
Yn bwrw'u hud drwy gig brau
A gwanwyn mewn ceginau.

LLEUCU LYNCH

Yn dy wên yn lledaenu, — yn yr hwyl
A'r awch am yfory,
Yn ddiatal o'th ddeutu,
Yno caf y golau cu.

CASI WYN

Na, nid gwybod y nodau — yw dy ran.
Rhoed i rai eneidiau
Y ddawn a'r angerdd i wau
O law Duw felodïau.

YR ATHRO DUNCAN TANNER

Yn ei waith roedd Cymru'n un, — yn ei ddysg
   Roedd ei waedd dros gyd-ddyn,
A'r hen daith dros freiniau dyn
Yn hawlio pob manylyn.

COFIO

Hirfaith yw gaeaf Arfon, — ond mi wn,
   Wedi maith dreialon,
Y daw lle y troediai hon
Yr hen dw' drwy'r drain duon.

I LLINOS WILLIAMS
AR EI HYMDDEOLIAD*

Rhai od iawn yw cewri dysg, — rhai di-weld
    Yw gwŷr doeth byd addysg;
    Y mae, mi wn, yn ein mysg
    Wymon a pherlau'n gymysg.

Dygwyd at ddysgedigion — un i'w dwyn
    Yn daer o'u helbulon;
    I fyd yn llawn ynfydion,
    I'w gwared hwy gyrrwyd hon.

Bu hon ym mhob trybini — a helynt
    Yn gynhaliaeth inni;
    Fe lanwodd ein ffurflenni,
    Rhoi trefn ar ein hanrhefn ni.

Nid oedd benbleth a'i llethai, — na, nid oedd
    Yr un dasg a'i lloriai;
    Os uchel yr anelai,
    Taro'r nod bob tro a wnâi.

Ni lunwyr ymchwil hynod, — lle awn-ni
    Heb Llinos i'n gwarchod?
    Awn yn ôl i fod yn od
    Ac i rincian, ni grancod!

---

* Prif weinyddwraig Coleg y Celfyddydau a'r Dyniaethau ym Mhrifysgol Bangor

I GOFIO
D. TECWYN LLOYD

Yn ei brint a'i draethu braf,— yn ei lên
    Sŵn ei lwyth a glywaf,
    Sŵn cae ar awr cynhaeaf
    A sŵn gwledd ar ddiwedd haf.

Yno mae'i Gymru uniaith, — yno o hyd
    O dan haul ei dalaith
    Mae wynebau dechrau'r daith
    Yn daer uwch eu pladurwaith.

Yno bydd eu byw a'u bod, — a'u hendir
    A llawnder eu taflod
    Yn rhoi i dreigl y rhod
    Ystyr er pob diflastod.

Un ei firi a'i Feirion, — un ei ddawn
    A phridd hen Edeirnion;
    Yn ei ddysg parhaodd hon
    Yn irlas ac ystyrlon.

Yn ei brint a'i draethu braf, — yn ei iaith
    Nid doethur a welaf,
    Ond llanc ar gae'r cynhaeaf
    Yno o hyd yn boddi'r haf.

ARCHIFDY *

I Einion Thomas, Archifydd Prifysgol Bangor,
ar ei ymddeoliad

Yno dan glo mae cof gwlad, — focs 'rôl bocs
 Lle bu dy ymroddiad
 Y mae'r pentyrrau'n dreftâd
 A'r heddwch yn wareiddiad.

Silff 'rôl silff nid papur sy, — nid hen lên
 Ond un wlad yn llechu,
 Un wlad mewn dogfennau lu
 A'i holl feirw'n llefaru.

Yno caf eu hing a'u cân — a'r oesau
 Yn croesi'r un llwyfan;
 Yno caf filflwydd cyfan,
 Heddiw a ddoe'n ddiwahân.

Yno fe glywaf gynion — ac araith,
 Rwy'n gweld gwerin Arfon
 A champau hardd a chwymp hon
 Yn nail ei hwythnosolion.

Ym mhrint brau yr angau'i hun — y mae'r bonc,
 Y mae'r byw ar ddibyn,
 Dagrau trasiedïau dyn
 A'i alar yn grychfelyn.

---

* Yn ystod ei gyfnod ym Mangor bu Einion yn gyfrifol am drefnu sawl arddangosfa yn seiliedig ar archifau'r Brifysgol, gan gynnwys un ar Streic Fawr y Penrhyn ac un arall am y Rhyfel Byd Cyntaf. Roedd hefyd yn un o sylfaenwyr Sefydliad Ymchwil Ystadau Cymru, sy'n tynnu ar gasgliad archifyddol helaeth Prifysgol Bangor yn y maes hwnnw.

Yno deil bechgyn Gwynedd — i rodio'n
        Gatrodau diddiwedd,
      A'r llun yn lifrai llynedd
      Yn galw'r bardd o glai'r bedd.

I'r hen wlad o'u huffern wleb — y daw'r rhain
        Gyda'r un sirioldeb;
      Daw'r rhain yn ôl o dir neb,
      I'r rhain fe roddir wyneb.

Rhoddaist i wlad ei gwreiddiau — fesul rhôl
        A didol ei stadau,
      A draw o gell daear gau
      Hel a didol dy dadau.

Yn llyfr rhent y llafur hir — dalennau
        Dy linach a welir,
      A glaw pob Awst a glywir
      Ynddo'n llethu teulu'r tir.

Rhoddaist i echdoe ruddiau, — sŵn a llais
        Yn holl lwch yr oesau;
      I go' rhoi cnawd a gïau
      A rhoi'r oll i ddoe barhau.

CYFARCH KATE ROBERTS YN 90 OED

Byw â'i henaid dan boenau — a wna hon
　　Yn nhŵr ei gofidiau,
　　Byw'n hirfaith dan arteithiau,
　　Byw'r ing sy'n bythol barhau.

Rhed cystrawen trueni — drwy ei haith,
　　Drwy ei hinc rhed cyni;
　　Hiraeth yw craidd ei stori,
　　Gwewyr yw ei geiriau hi.

LADA*

Araf oedd y milltiroedd, — ie, araf
    Er gwario'r holl gannoedd;
    Lada ar y diawl ydoedd,
    Ond un da mewn eira oedd.

Lada'r lefftis a'r tlodion, — un Lada
    Clywadwy ei biston;
    Un â'i fwg o Fynwy i Fôn,
    Un Lada'n llawn dyledion.

Dduw Iôr, pa ryw ddihiryn — a dwyllodd
    Y dall â'r fath recsyn?
    Ei anrhydedd, yr adyn,
    Yw dêl wael i'w deulu'i hun.

O Dduw, pan ddaw ei ddiwedd, — un llinell
    Hynod o gynghanedd
    Yn fawl a gaiff ar ei fedd:
    "Y rhwd oedd ei anrhydedd".

* Un o'r ceir cyntaf a fu yn fy meddiant. Fe'i prynais gan fy mrawd yng nghyfraith a'm perswadiodd y byddai'r system grancio â llaw a oedd iddo o fantais fawr mewn stormydd eira.

Y GANRIF FWYAF

(I gyfarch Hywel Teifi Edwards
yn ei gyfrol deyrnged)

Rhoesom ein collfarn arni
A'n sen ar ei rhodres hi.
Ein rhan fu gwatwar o hyd
Ei hawdlau cloff a rhydlyd.
Gwae iaith chwyddedig ei gwŷr,
Gwae hwythau, ei beirdd-bregethwyr.

Hyglyw oedd ei hunan-glod
A dwndwr ei Phrydeindod,
A'i hynfydus steddfodau
Yn drwch o wladgarwch gau.
Un wlad orseddol ydoedd,
Hon a'i barddas syrcas oedd.

Rhoesom ein collfarn arni
Ac o'n co' ei halltudio hi,
A chael drwy goleg a chwaeth
Nodded mewn gwir lenyddiaeth
A thyfu i brydyddu'n braff
Â gwirgrefft mewn gwiw orgraff.

✳

Yna storm, cyrhaeddaist ti
I ddiawlio'r cyfryw ddwli
A'n galw, bawb, o'n gŵyl bob ha'
I ŵyl ryfeddol Gwalia.
Â'i hanes ein dihuno
A chwalu'r cen uwchlaw'r co'.

Hon ganrif â'n barn arni,
Ei hwyl a'i stomp 'welaist ti
A chlais ei Llyfrau Gleision
Yma ar wedd y Gymru hon,
A dwndwr ei Phrydeindod
Yn un baich yn nwfn ein bod.

Er bod ein collfarn arni,
Mynnu 'wnest mai'i phlant ŷm ni;
Ni yw llwyth ei chôr a'i llên,
Lluoedd ei phwll a'i hawen;
Epil ŷm i gapel hon
Ac i glwb ei beirdd gwlybion!

Merêd, daw'n wyliau eto

Ni rwydwyd yr ehedydd

AR FEDD MEREDYDD EVANS

Merêd, daw'n wyliau eto; — daw rhywrai
    Drwy'r eira i byncio.
    Ai rhy gryf fydd bolltau'r gro?
    A yw'r gân yn gryg yno?

"I eraill gyda'r Fari — y daw'r hwyl
    Boptu'r drws eleni,
    Ond o'i ddatgloi fe glywi
    Drwy'u lleisiau hwy fy llais i."

AR FEDD EI ŴYR, GARETH MCLOUGHLIN

Ni rwydwyd yr ehedydd. — Oni chlywch
    Ei lef ar y mynydd
    A phelydryn derfyn dydd
    Yn dân ar ei adenydd?

Un hwyr trodd y môr o'r traeth.
Un hwyr bu farw hiraeth.

I GOFIO CISSIE MORRIS, ABERDARON*

Nid oedd cysgod lle rhodiai, — na galar
    A'i gilwg lle troediai;
    Yr oedd tangnefedd lle'r âi,
    Hindda a heulwen pan ddelai.

Pan loywai hi'r gwmnïaeth, — ni welem
    Dreialon marwolaeth;
    Rhoi'r hwyr i borthi'r hiraeth,
    Rhoi'r nos i'w galar a wnaeth.

Hon serchog, heulog ei gwedd, — hon ysig
    Pan ddôi'r nos i'w hannedd,
    Hon yn nhonnau'i hanhunedd,
    Hon drwy'r hwyr ar draeth di-hedd.

Yno rhwng y dwfn a'r rhos — pwy a ŵyr
    Pa ing sydd i'r cyfnos?
    Ac yn nhŷ unig y nos
    Y mae'r eigion mor agos.

Ond rhyddhad rhyw hwyr a ddaeth — a chiliodd
    O'i chalon bob alaeth;
    Un hwyr trodd y môr o'r traeth,
    Un hwyr bu farw hiraeth.

Un nos deg a diystŵr — i'w hannedd
    Daeth yr hen gyfannwr;
    Ar awr gêl, rhwng gwraig a'i gŵr,
    Fe fu'r angau'n gyfryngwr.

---

* Bu farw yn 88 oed yn 2015. Roedd ei gŵr, John Morris, yn brifathro Ysgol Gynradd Aberdaron. Bu farw yn 1977 wrth iddo geisio achub un o'i ddisgyblion o'r môr. Bu farw ei hunig fab, y newyddiadurwr Dylan Morris, yn annhymig yn 1996, a chollodd ei hŵyr Liam mewn amgylchiadau trist.

ARCHEOLEGWYR GEIRIAU *

*(I Ann, Llinos, Morfydd a Nerys,
ac i gofio am Caerwyn a Geraint)*

I'r afael â'r canrifoedd — yr aethom;
 Er mai rhwth y llysoedd,
  O air i air mynd lle'r oedd
  Hen drysor dan dw'r oesoedd.

Hawlio 'wnaem yr olion hyn, — hawlio'u sain
 Fesul sill ac englyn
  A chael dan ysgall a chwyn
  Warineb fesul gronyn.

O fieri, llafariaid — a dynnem
 A doniau penceirddiaid;
  Rhyddhau llên o bridd a llaid,
  Gogrwn sŵn hen gytseiniaid.

'Maflyd â rhyw fyd a fu — a wnaethom
 A thrwy'n hiaith ei gyrchu.
  Ai rhy glòs y brigau lu
  I ddynion ei feddiannu?

---

* Lluniwyd fersiwn gynharaf y gerdd hon ar gais Yr Athro Dafydd Johnston, a hynny
i ddathlu ugainmlwyddiant sefydlu'r Ganolfan Uwchefrydiau Cymreig a Cheltaidd yn
1985. Prosiect academaidd cyntaf y Ganolfan oedd darparu'r golygiad modern cyntaf o
holl waith Beirdd y Tywysogion. Yr oeddwn i, a'r rhai a enwir uchod, yn aelodau o'r tîm
a ymgymerodd â'r dasg honno.

O gam i gam yno i'n gŵydd — deuai drain
     Cystrawennau afrwydd,
    A'r awch i ildio oedd rwydd
    Yng ngwe efrau'r anghofrwydd.

Ond eto roedd yno ddau — yn rhoi ias
     Wrth droi'r drysi'n awdlau,
    Yn ennyn ynom ninnau
    Y wefr o weld dalen frau.

At rwndwal y tair talaith — y'n galwyd,
     Ac o'u hawlio'r eilwaith,
    Cawsom yno hawlio'u hiaith
    A memrynau'u mireinwaith.

GWLAD Y GLO *

Nid yw gwlad lychlyd y glo — mwy i'w gweld,
    Ond mae gan bob Cymro
    Rhyw gwm yn nyfnder ei go'
    A hanes ei lwyth yno.

Hon yw gwlad yr hen g'ledi — a'i haliers
    Draw o'r haul yn rhegi;
    I rai Samaria yw hi
    Yn hanner perthyn inni.

Ond i ti y mae'n dreftâd, — ei hanes
    Yn un â'th wneuthuriad;
    Ei düwch sy'n dy wead,
    I'w stori hi wyt barhad.

Di-iaith yw'r holl siafftiau du — a gefaist
    Yn dy gof yn llechu;
    Ond cwm a phwll a thad-cu
    Ydyw'r hedd o'i fydryddu.

Y mae eigionau'n dy gân, — daeareg
    Cyfandiroedd cyfan
    A'u glo hwy yn gnepyn glân
    O ddwfn Annwfn ei hunan.

Ac un dyn a weli'n dod — draw o'r haul
    A'i drem drwy'r anwybod,
    Mesur ei gamau isod
    Drwy y baw hyd odre bod.

---

* I gyfarch Jason Walford Davies ar ennill Coron yr Eisteddfod Genedlaethol
yn 2004. Lluniwyd ei gerdd *Egni* er cof am ei dad-cu, Brinley Powell, ac i gofio
am Streic y Glowyr, 1984–5.

Arwr heb ei Aneirin; — trwy ei oes
     Yng Nghatraeth ei werin
    Dram wrth dram y dôi ei drin,
    Ddydd 'rôl dydd ei Ododdin.

Yna o'i gwman fe gamai, — ac o gad
     Y cysgodion ciliai;
    Dod yn ôl yn dad a wnâi,
    Yn ŵr i'r wraig a'i carai.

Un wyneb yn troi'n gannoedd, — un yrfa
     Yn yrfa'r holl filoedd,
    Ei gwm yn rhes o gymoedd,
    A'i aelwyd wâr – ein gwlad oedd.

A'u glo hwy yn gnepyn glân

O ddwfn Annwfn ei hunan.

MYRDDIN 1939–45*

Fe wyddom oll am feddau — yr hogiau
    A rhegwn eu hangau;
    Wylwn lle bu'r magnelau
    Yn bwrw'r haf o'u cyrff brau.

Yng ngraean traethau'r glanio, — yn yr Aifft,
    Lle mae Rhein yn llifo,
    Mae rhyw ran o lwch fy mro,
    Llond bedd o Wynedd yno.

Ond y groes oedd goroesi — i eraill
    Ac osgoi'r bwledi;
    Ofer yw arwrol fri
    A'r enaid yn cynrhoni.

Heb fedd lle bu ei fyddin, — yno â'i bang
    Ymhob oes bydd Myrddin;
    Rhoi ei enaid i'w frenin,
    Nid rhoi'i waed a wna mewn trin.

Nid oriau mo'i Arfderydd; — yn ei gwsg
    Hi yw'r gad na dderfydd;
    Drwy ei ben yn ffrwydro bydd
    Dur a gïau'n dragywydd.

Gwêl heddiw o'i Gelyddon, — ymhell bell
    O'r byd a'i ymryson,
    Fôr di-drai y frwydr hon,
    A gwêl heddiw goluddion.

Hen glwyf yn ei glai a lŷn, — un na wêl
    Llygad noeth ei gyd-ddyn;
    Y briw na wêl y gelyn
    Yw'r anaf dyfnaf mewn dyn.

---

* I gyfarch Jerry Hunter am ennill y Fedal Ryddiaith yn Eisteddfod Genedlaethol 2010. Roedd ei nofel *Gwenddydd* yn ailadrodd chwedl Myrddin yng nghyd-destun yr Ail Ryfel Byd.

ADDASIAD O SONED 104
GAN SHAKESPEARE

Nid wyf yn dy weled di
Un ennyd mewn penwynni.
Yn harddwych, lle y cerddi,
Tu hwnt i henaint wyt ti.

Ond fe ddaeth tro'r tymhorau
Wedi awr ein serch ni'n dau.
Aeth tri haf yn aeaf oer
A'u hwyrnosau'n farn iasoer.
Fe ddaeth tri hydref gan ddwyn
Trwy gynnwrf ein tri gwanwyn,
A Mehefin i grino
Irder iach Ebrill ar dro.

Yn araf, araf, o hyd
Ni welaf, fy anwylyd,
Ddafn rôl dafn dy harddwch di
Yn dy wên yn dihoeni
A'n heinioes yn ronynnau
O dywod rhwng dwylo dau.

Ai twyll 'wêl y llygaid hyn?
A dreisiwyd hud y rhosyn?

Chwithau'r rhai sydd yma i ddod,
Ofer, ofer eich dyfod
A bydd cyn eich dod i'r byd
Eich hafau yn llwch hefyd.

Y DDWYGERDD AGOS*
(*I Gwennant Pyrs, ac i Gôr Seiriol yn 25 oed*)

Yn neuaddau'n llenyddiaeth,
Yn nhai gwin yr awen gaeth
Dwy ddawn yn gyfrodedd oedd,
Hwy a asiwyd drwy'r oesoedd.
I lên fe roed telynau
Ac i gainc rhoed cerdd i'w gwau;
Dwy hen grefft yn gadwyn gron
A dwy hŷn na chof dynion.

Heb dannau roedd geiriau gynt
Yn weddwon. Mor wag oeddynt.
Roedd i air ei gerddoriaeth,
Roedd ceinciau i'w geiriau'n gaeth.
A gwae fardd, mor gryg ei fyd,
Anafus ei gân hefyd:
Ni ddôi gwefr i'r byrddau gwin
O'i gywydd heb ddeg ewin.
Rhyw edau ungor ydoedd,
Onid iaith heb enaid oedd?

Yn neuaddau'n llenyddiaeth
Newydd win i ni a ddaeth,
Ac i lys Cymreig y wledd
Fe roed yr hen frwdfrydedd
Am fod tafod a nodau
Yma o hyd yn ymwáu
A rhai â'r reddf, fel yr oedd,
I asio crefftau'r oesoedd.

---

* Lewys Daron, wrth iddo gyfeirio at feistrolaeth y bardd Tudur Aled ar grefftau cerdd
dafod a cherdd dant, piau'r ymadrodd *y ddwygerdd agos*.

Ynot ti mae holl dreftâd
Ddoe ein hawen ddiwnïad,
Ac ynot mae clymau clòs
Y ddwygerdd waraidd, agos.
Yn dy gôr mae'r grefft i gyd
A'r hyn fu yn troi'n fywyd.

Gosodaist ti gerddi gant
Ac o'u gosod fe gawsant
Rymuster llif ar Ferwyn
A llyfnder fel llyfnder llyn.
Weithiau trwy gyweiriau'r gân
Gweryra gaea'r Aran.
Yno â'i balm hefyd bydd
Lliw ei hun ar bnawn llonydd,
Ac o ddafn i ddafn fe ddaw
Yno i hawlio'r gyfalaw
Rhyw rin sy'n hŷn na'r heniaith,
Dimensiwn tu hwnt i iaith.

A holl rif eu llawryfon
A'u bri hwy yn falchder bron,
A oes ryw her sy ar ôl
O greu sêr o Gôr Seiriol?

Yr her o hyd yw parhau
I fynnu'r uchelfannau,
I yngan â'r hen angerdd,
I wau'r gainc yn un â'r gerdd.
Yr her yw rhoi, rhoi o raid,
Yr hyn sy'n nwfn yr enaid,
A hawlio'r wefr fel yr oedd
Drwy asio crefftau'r oesoedd.

I DDATHLU PEN-BLWYDD
MAIR YN 50 OED *

Y Fair wen sy'n y nef fry,
Hi a roes im yr Iesu;
Rhoi nefol Frenin hefyd
A baban bach sydd ben byd.
Â'i hennaint ym Methania
I'w ŵydd Ef daeth ail Fair dda.
Hi â'i nard fu'n Ei lanhau,
Yn iro Ei flinderau.
Wrth fedd gwag, Mair fam Iago
Hithau a ddaeth i'w ŵydd o,
A'r trydydd dydd ato daeth
Fair arall fawr ei hiraeth,
Y Fagdlen ddall gan drallod,
Hon y Fair na wyddai fod
Ei Duw yn siarad â hi, —
Iôr heb anaf, Rabbwni.

Ym mhob gwlad yn glywadwy
I'r pedair Mair caner mwy.
Ond y mae o hyd i mi
Un arall i'w chlodfori.
Yn fynych yn fy henoed
I Wynedd af yn ddi-oed.
Yno beunos heb anair
Dof o hyd i'r bumed Fair.
Hi yw cannwyll Nanconwy,
Hi yw fflam ei phlas a'i phlwy.
Yn fardd llwm caf rodd a lles
A gwleddoedd gan f'arglwyddes.
Mae imi lys rhag storm wleb
A thân lle bo'i doethineb.

---

* Mair Parry-Jones yw Pennaeth y Gwasanaeth Cyfieithu a Chofnodi Seneddol
yng Nghynulliad Cenedlaethol Cymru. Rhyw ymdrech sydd yn rhan gyntaf y cywydd
i efelychu dulliau cyfeiriadol y Cywyddwyr gynt o ganu i wragedd a merched.

Ym Morgannwg, mawr gynnydd,
Draw o Wynedd senedd sydd.
Yno daw y craff a'r doeth,
Rhai o rinwedd, rhai annoeth,
Rhai o werth, ac ambell rôg
I rantio yn hirwyntog.
Drwy y rhain un llais a draidd
Yn dyner o sidanaidd,
A thôn ei chyfieithu hi
Amdanynt yn ymdonni,
A chwa ddiymdrech ei hiaith
Yn dawel wyrth rhwng dwyiaith;
Hon â'i geirio hardd-gywrain,
Hon gystrawen gymen, gain,
Yn rhoi i'w hiaith drystfawr hwy
Eneiniad o Nanconwy.

Am wyrth ei chyfieithu mwy
Caner i Fair Nanconwy.
Am win hael ei chwmni hi
Rhodder diolchgar weddi;
A bydd beunydd heb anair
O hyd fawl i'r bumed Fair.

ALUN FFRED JONES

(Ar ei ymddeoliad fel Aelod Cynulliad Arfon)

Nid ystrydeb bocs sebon — yw dy gêm,
        Nid gwag addewidion;
        Rhy hawdd yn y Gymru hon
        Yw hau hadau breuddwydion.

I fwriad y llefari, — â rheswm
        Nid brys y gweithredi;
        Mae hid yn d'addewid di,
        Fe wêl hon ei chyflawni.

Yn y Bae mae rhuthr y byd — yn un don,
        Ond y doeth sydd hefyd
        Yn cofio yno o hyd
        Nad y Bae ydyw bywyd.

Dy yrfa 'roed i Arfon, — ni, rywfodd,
        A hawliodd dy galon,
        Ni filoedd o ofalon,
        Y ni o hyd piau hon.

MARWNAD GWYN THOMAS

Draw i Ŵyr, drwy Eryri,
Mae siom lle tramwyais i.
Yn nhai dysg cyfeillion da
Galarus fy holl glera.
Ni fu flinach dwy flynedd,
Ni ddôi fis heb newydd fedd.
O angladd i angladd es
Â meinwynt yn fy mynwes.

A fynni di fwy, ein Duw?
Dy gnwd, ai digon ydyw?
Eto fyth o Went i Fôn
A fwyelli 'nghyfeillion?
Fe hawliaist dy siâr filwaith,
Ai sigo dysg yw dy waith?
A fynni'n llwyr ddifa'n llên
A daearu pob derwen?

Ni'r diniwed, ni chredem,
'Rôl profi braw dy law lem,
Eto o hyd y mynnet ti
Un arall o'r hen gewri.
Ond dy law diatal yw,
Wyt eiddig eto heddiw,
A'r un siom i'm siwrnai sydd
I ryw ran o Feirionnydd.

---

* Cyfeirir yn y llinellau agoriadol at y colledion dirifedi a ddioddefodd y byd llenyddol
Cymraeg yn ystod yr ychydig flynyddoedd cyn i Gwyn Thomas farw. Collwyd Nigel
Jenkins, Gerallt Lloyd Owen, James Nicholas, John Davies, Meredydd Evans, John
Rowlands, Bryan Martin Davies, Harri Pritchard Jones ac R. Geraint Gruffydd
yn y cyfnod hwnnw.

Aed beirdd byd i bridd y bedd,
Aed eu hawen i'w diwedd.
Marw yw Gwyn. Marw'r gân.

Aed beirdd byd i bridd y bedd,
Aed eu hawen i'w diwedd.
Marw yw Gwyn. Marw'r gân.
Fe gefaist, Dduw, dy gyfan.
Gyrrer geiriau i'r gweryd
A'u grym a'u hawch i'r gro mud.
Rhodder taw ar gystrawen,
Rhodder iaith i'r ddaear hen.

✳

Ei bobl oedd ei barabl o,
Yr oedd eu gwydnwch drwyddo.
Yn nhraw ei lafar o hyd
Un dre' fu drwy ei fywyd,
A hyd eithaf ei dafod,
Faen wrth faen o ddwfn ei fod,
Un dre' oedd ei gystrawen
A'i thai llwyd yn weithiau llên,
Un dref a'i dwndwr hefyd
Yno i fardd yn troi'n fyd.

Haenau'r glaw ar greigleoedd,
Haul a niwl y Blaenau oedd.
Ni waeth pa le yr aethai
Yr oedd y Blaenau lle'r âi,
Roedd agorydd ei geiriau,
Roedd yno'r ddawn i'w rhyddhau,
Roedd dillad gwaith ei hiaith hi,
Y pylor a'r capeli,
Ac yno ymhob genyn
Roedd clymau'i doeau mor dynn.

Y stryd a'i stori ydoedd
A baich ein meidroldeb oedd,
Yr ofn drwy ein cnawd a red,
Yr eco ar fat criced,
Y Farilyn loywlun lân
A Chulhwch a Chwhwlan,
Oesau llên ein sgwrsio llon
A geiriau plant ac wyrion,
Y cof a oedd Feibl cyfan,
Y stori gomig ar gân,
Yr hwyl wrth i ddau neu dri
O hogiau ddod gan regi
A dwyn holl sgriffiadau'r dydd
Heb wewyr o Gwm Bowydd:
Hyn oedd Gwyn, hyn oedd ei gân,
Fe gefaist, Dduw, dy gyfan.

Ac o'n byd wrth gymryd Gwyn
Fe hawliaist y ddau Foelwyn,
Dwyn cordeddog goediog wâl
Y cynfyd yng nghwm Cynfal,
Yna mynd â sinemâu
Ein llynedd lle dôi lluniau
Yr anfad â barn arnynt
Ar Sadyrnau'r gynnau gynt
A rhyw un yn dod o raid
I gynnal cefn y gweiniaid.

Est â rîl y stori hon
O Amerig tir Meirion.
Est â Gwyn. Fe est â'i gân
O'n gafael, chwalu'n gyfan
Ym môr heli marwolaeth
Ôl ei droed ar feddal draeth.
Dwyn Gwyn, Dduw, o'i fyw a'i fod
I fôr enfawr ei anfod.

✻

Rhwydd im dy geryddu, Dduw
Di-hid, am un nad ydyw.
Ond eto, eto, mi wn
Pe chwalai'r clai, pe'i clyw-wn
A'i weled, na cheid wedyn
Un gair i'th ddwrdio gan Gwyn.
Cans dyn ei hun yn ddi-wâd
Fu awdur ei ddifodiad
A'i angau, ac ef hefyd
Piau awr y cwymp o hyd.

Yn ei go', ymhob gewyn,
Yn ei gân fe wyddai Gwyn
Nad rhyw rith oedd traha'i hil
Na rhu bostfawr y bwystfil.
Nid hen lên ein beiblau oedd
Na straeon mewn festrïoedd.

Un nawn hir, ac ef yn iau,
Oni welodd y riliau
Yn dyfod fel edefyn
Draw o siambrau angau'i hun,
A'r esgyrn noeth drwy'r sgrin wen
Yn dileu pob chwedl lawen?
Lle dôi rhyw gowboi â gwn,
I wylo daeth chwe miliwn.
Lun wrth lun, y bwystfil hen
A droediodd drwy ei Eden.

✻

O weld ôl difaol dyn,
Pwy a wadai'r cwymp wedyn?
Drwy'r blynyddoedd roedd o raid
Hen drueni drwy'i enaid
A hen gystudd yn cuddio
Dan ei stori gomig o.
Hanner yn hanner â'i hwyl
Yr oedd awr ddu ei arwyl;
Yn ei awen hen aeaf
Hanner yn hanner â haf.

Ond rhywfodd, o'r anoddun
Dua' oll lle plymiodd dyn,
I ŵydd Gwyn fe ddôi bedd gwag
A dôi yno Dduw dinag.
Yno roedd Gethsemane,
Yno o hyd roedd teyrnas ne'.
Fe welai ef olau hon,
A'i weled yn ei galon.

A rhywfodd, o'r anoddun
Dua' oll lle rhempiai dyn,
Fe wyddai fod celfyddyd
Yn drech na'r dyfnder o hyd,
Na allai'r hen dywyllwch
Hawlio'i lên yn un â'i lwch,
Na roir geiriau i'r gweryd
Na'u grym a'u hawch i'r gro mud.
A gwyddai fesul gweddi,
Ni waeth am ein dwrdio ni,
Na fyn Duw ddifa un dyn
Na'i hawlio fel hen elyn.
Duw o hyd bywyd ydyw,
A Duw ei hun cariad yw.

PILLGWENLLY

CERDD FACH SEML

Sŵn carolau'n llenwi'r tŷ
A'r nos yn ddu tu allan,
A minnau eto ar drothwy hwyl
A gŵyl y baban bychan
Yn cofio'r Nadoligau gynt
A'r rhai nad ydynt yma.

Y mwstwr yn yr oriau mân
Ar ŵyl y baban bychan,
A chyffro'r plant yn llenwi'r tŷ
A'r nos yn ddu tu allan,
A minnau'n cofio'r cyffro gynt
A'r rhai nad ydynt yma.

Llawenydd gwledd yn llenwi'r tŷ
A'r gwynt yn gry' tu allan
A ninnau'n codi'n gwydrau glân
Ar ŵyl y baban bychan
Gan gofio'r gwleddoedd a fu gynt
A'r rhai nad ydynt yma.